Grace Thoughts

A Handbook To Help, Encourage and Brighten Your Life

by

Morris J. St. Angelo

Empyrion Publishing
Winter Garden, FL

Grace Thoughts
Copyright © 2014 by Morris J. St. Angelo

ISBN: 978-0692251331

Empyrion Publishing
PO Box 784327
Winter Garden, FL
Info@EmpyrionPublishing.com

Unless otherwise noted, all Scripture quotations are from the New International Version of the Bible.

King James Version is noted as KJV
New King James is noted as NKJ
New American Standard is noted as NAS
English Standard Version is noted as ESV
Amplified Version is noted as AMP
The Message is noted as MSG
God's Word Translation is noted as GWT

All rights reserved. No part of this book may be reproduced, stored in a retrieval system, or transmitted in any form or by any means - electronic, mechanical, photocopy, recording, or any other, without permission in writing from the author.

Printed in the United States of America

Endorsements

I have known Morris St Angelo for many years. He has been a pursuer of truth since I have known him and his lovely family. In recent years, Morris has realized, in fuller measure as I, what the grace of God through Christ's finished work has mightily accomplished. As a result, he has reengaged in ministry at deeper and more powerful ways than before. Frankly, that is what truth does to pastors. Morris's new book, Grace Thoughts, is a welcomed and needed addition to the growing library of "grace truths" being published today.

Clark Whitten
Lead Pastor
Grace Church of Greater Orlando
Author of *Pure Grace*

Pastor St. Angelo is a loving and sincere man of God. His involvement in the community of the City of Slidell extends across every denomination. People in the area have shared with me that the weekly articles Pastor St. Angelo writes in the "Slidell Independent" have made an impact on them. They often feel that because his articles open with something that most everyone can relate to or imagine, the message that follows gives a lasting reflection. (These articles are the basis of the book you are about to read)... Pastor

St. Angelo is a valued member of our community and the City of Slidell is fortunate to have him to reap the benefits of his passion for enhancing the lives of the people in our area and improving the community.

Freddy Drennan
Mayor
City of Slidell

One of the joys of knowing Pastor Morris for many, many years is that I have watched him experience God's grace in an incredible way. He has received God's grace. He walks in God's grace, and he gives God's grace. Grace works.

Allen Hickman
Lead Pastor
Resurrection Life Church
Picayune, Mississippi

Anyone confused about God's existence should meet my friend Morris. Some pastors preach. Morris lives. Jesus walks around with real hands and feet because He lives in Morris. I have been blessed to witness and grow in the simplicity and awe of God's grace through life with my mentor and friend. My prayer has long been for God to bless other men with a Morris of their own. That prayer has been answered in the form of this book. Need a great book on business, love, relationships, being a man, dealing with disaster and joy? This is it. I've witnessed Jesus in real life with Morris. Now you can too. Enjoy!

Arthur Knapp
Business Associate and Friend
Orlando, Florida

Morris St. Angelo goes by many names and titles. Some include Mario, Reverend, Pastor, Brother, Husband, Son, Friend, Preacher, Author, Counselor. Whichever you choose is most likely true. He is an authentic friend. He is a Preacher of the truth about Jesus. He seeks and gives wise counsel. To me, he is the example of God's unconditional love and favor. I call him "Pop."

Tiffany Lobo
Author of Big Good God and Little Busy Izzy
Winter Garden, FL

When the Lord thought of Morris He knew that a young woman named Stacey would need his protection, loyalty, wisdom and affirmation. He knew the journey that would place us in the same time and space and He created Morris' heart in His own image.... a heart of understanding, gratitude and determination. I've witnessed, over and over, this eternal heart and know the power Morris has to influence and encourage the Lord's creation... His beloved humanity, whom He adores without measure. In this book, filled with great hope, faith and love, Morris pens his eternal expectations. His heart towards mankind is forever welcoming... proclaiming "All IS well. Come home." This book will encourage many and will lift the eyes of the broken hearted... to see themselves as Jesus has always seen them... forever in the conversation and heart of the Trinity. We've always belonged. Enjoy Morris' heart. :)

Stacy Sorensen
Grace Sister and Friend
Atlanta, Georgia

What a great idea for a book! Grace Thoughts is a compilation of spiritual and practical writings from the pen of Morris St. Angelo, a prolific creator of timely and thoughtful writings based on the beauty of the gospel. Filled with insight and wit on numerous topics, "Grace Thoughts" is indexed by words and Bible verses, and can easily be used as a devotional. I count Morris as an honest and gracious friend, and it's my pleasure to endorse his book.

Rick Manis
Author and Speaker
Rick Manis Ministries
Winter Garden, Florida

I wholeheartedly recommend this new book by Morris St. Angelo. Enjoy the words in this book like a good meal and ponder them in your heart. Morris knows Jesus and his desire is to make His King known to all who thirst for true life. This is no ordinary book for it contains a revelation that will carry you to another reality in Christ while you walk this earth.

James Barron
Attorney at Law
Grace Teacher and Friend
Longwood, Florida

Dedication

This book is dedicated to my wife Pat and my daughter Tiffany.

To Pat because she is my co-everything. As husband and wife we've fulfilled the biblical admonition that the two would become one. She gives her life so that I can do things like write this book.

Tiffany is my encourager. She's been directing my life since the day she was born. I couldn't get myself together on this book until she grabbed the reins and pushed me. In days she had the articles being edited by her friends and started creating the design of the book. I just did whatever she told me to do.

Thanks Pat and Tiff. 1-4-3

Table of Contents

Forward	i
How To Use This Book	v
A Beautiful Day	1
A Beautiful Life	4
Abortion and the Constitution	7
Accepted by God	10
America and Spiritual Freedom	12
Ancient Deities in Modern Times	15
Awe Filled Church	17
Baptism of the Holy Spirit	19
Be Thankful	22
Bible and School	24
Black Robe Regiment	27
Blessings	30
Broken People	32
Choosing to Avoid Evil	35
Christmas and Memories	37
Day of Prayer	40
Dead in Christ are Alive	43
Depression	45
Desertion and Despair	48
Directions	51
DNA and Decisions	54
Doldrums and Boredoms	57

Doors of Direction	**60**
Easter	**62**
Easter Bunny Prayer	**64**
End of Tine	**66**
End Times	**69**
Enemies	**72**
Evidence of Jesus	**74**
Family Values	**77**
Fasting	**80**
Father's Day	**82**
Feelings	**85**
First Commandment	**89**
Follow His Voice	**91**
Forgiveness Bucket List	**94**
Founding Father's Prayers	**96**
Fragrances Have Meaning To Us	**99**
Freedom	**101**
Freedom of Speech	**104**
Friends	**107**
Fruitfulness	**110**
Giving, Tithes and Taxes	113
Glory and Beauty	115
God Cares For You	118
God Is Very Near You	120
God Orders Your Steps	123
God's Plan For You	125
God's Plan vs Yours	127

Good Friday	129
Gospel to Rome	131
Government and Elections	134
Government and Taxes	137
Grace and Rest	140
Groundhog Day and Forgiveness	143
Guarantees	145
Have You Been Born Again?	147
Have You Seen Any Angels Lately?	149
Heaven Destination	152
Heaven's Crown	154
Helpless	156
Holiday Season	158
Holidays Are Coming	161
Holy Week	163
How the Blind Can See	165
Hurricane Katrina	168
Hyper-Grace	171
Imaginations	174
Important Things	177
Independence Day and Black Robe Regiment	180
Integrity	183
Jesus is Alive	185
Kingdom of God	188
Leadership	190
Learning to Live	193
Liberty Has a Price	195

Life is a Vapor	198
Loneliness	200
Long Life	202
Love and Marriage	204
Mardi Gras and Sin	206
Marriage and Love	208
Memorial Day	211
Mind of Christ	213
Mother's Day	216
Murder	218
New Year's Resolutions	221
Noah and the Ark	224
Power	227
Praise to God	230
Prayer	232
Pre-Incarnate Christ	234
Proof of the Resurrection	236
Pure Grace	239
Refreshing	241
Rejoice	243
Rest and Thanks	246
Revival	248
Sacrifice	251
Saints	253
Salvation and Perfection	255
Salvation From Sin	258
Shaking the Kingdom	261

Sheep and Pastors	263
Sin and Jelly Bellies	265
Sorrow and Tragedy	267
Soul Salvation	269
Tear Down Wall Street	272
Ten Commandments	275
Thanks to Founding Fathers	277
Thanksgiving	280
The End of a Terrorist	283
The Way to Walk	286
There Is Hope For You	289
Thoughts	292
True Love	294
Trust God	296
Unshakable Kingdom	299
Valentine's Day	301
Validation	303
Waiting on God	305
War on 9/11	308
Weak Made Strong	310
Weapons of Warfare	312
What Does The Future Hold?	314
What If Heaven Were Closed Today?	317
When You Fall	320
Worry	323
Worthy	326
You Still Have Value	328

Key Word Index	**331**
Scripture Index	**343**
About The Author	**351**

Forward

How precious are your thoughts about me, O God. They cannot be numbered! I can't even count them; they outnumber the grains of sand!
(Psalms 139:17-18 NLT)

"Grace Thoughts" is exactly that – thoughts. One of my seminary professors wrote a book and titled it "Thinking about God." He said that theology is a combination of two words – God and Thinking. He concluded that theology simply means to think about God. I've thought a lot about that over the years, but mostly I've thought about what God was thinking about. What's on His mind? What are His thoughts?

I was invited by the owner of my hometown's weekly newspaper to write an article for the Inspirational page of his brand-new publication. He wanted to make sure that there was an ample supply of Good News to encourage the community amid all the bad news. I thought it would be a one week one time endeavor. That was on January 2, 2009 and I have written an article for every issue of the newspaper since then. That's a lot of thoughts.

To my great surprise folks seem to like the articles. At first, my friends were telling me they enjoyed the weekly thoughts. But soon people I would meet, who I didn't know, were saying they were reading the articles and benefiting from them. I've been told that people save them, cut them out and send them to friends who might find them beneficial, and some even use them to teach devotional groups. I must admit I am humbled by it all.

The idea of putting some of these writings into book form came from a friend. He suggested that it would be a blessing if people could use the book to help, encourage or brighten their lives. I'm all about encouraging people so I decided to publish this book.

My biggest task was to name it something that would describe its contents. I thought about "Newspaper Articles" but that sounded trite. I liked "Thinking about God," but maybe people would think it was about yoga or transcendental meditations. I thought about it and tried a few titles on my family and every title got a negative response. Then I remembered what I do each week before I write an article. I ask God what He would like to say? And He gives me a "thought." I take that God thought and start clicking away on my keyboard. And so I thought it would be accurate to name it "God's Thoughts." But that sounds like I might think I'm God. Then it hit me. I'm all about Grace! I believe in Jesus and what He's done with no help from me. So the final title is "Grace Thoughts" because that's exactly what they are. I pray that you are encouraged by this book to think about God. His thoughts are the only reason this book exists. And in case you hadn't thought about it – He's always thinking about you.

Morris J. St. Angelo

How To Use This Book

This book is designed to encourage you and assist you in the everyday events of life. Each chapter is a Grace Thought about an emotion, an issue, a time of joy or a valley of sorrow. Just peruse the chapter names until you find one that captures your imagination or meets your need.

In the rear of the book is a cross reference of a multitude of key words and/or topics of Grace Thoughts that you might be searching for. You will find that a particular key word may be examined and explored in several different chapters. Each Grace Thought topic shows the corresponding page numbers where you can find it throughout the book.

A second cross reference has every scripture that is used in the book and the page number of where you will find them. This way you can search for a particular idea found in Scripture that you want to find and explore.

The goal of *Grace Thoughts* is to give you a reference handbook that can be used in everyday situations to inspire you and lead you to what God and His Grace has to say to you.

A Beautiful Day

The 1955 movie, based on the stage play "Oklahoma," begins with a scene that sets the tempo for the rest of the movie. Gordon MacRae is riding his horse through a wheat field and bellows out in song the lyrics, "Oh, what a beautiful morning. Oh, what a beautiful day. I've got a wonderful feeling, everything's going my way." What a great way to begin a movie. What a great way to begin a day. As the movie progresses you soon learn that maybe everything is not as rosy as Gordon would lead you to believe. The leading lady is playing hard to get. The villain is addicted to porn and has his eye on the leading lady. MacRae has no job and the only thing he owns is his horse and gun. And there is a range war between the farmers and the cattlemen. Yikes, this sounds like normal life today! How can a leading man be so happy with so much trouble brewing all around? Easy, it's a movie.

But what about real life? Are we supposed to live our lives in the stark reality that everything is not always beautiful? The answer is absolutely not! God has a way of turning our worst day into our best day if we just look for Him in the middle of our situations.

King David wrote words of encouragement in the Psalms: "Weeping may last through the night, but joy comes with the morning." (Psalms 30:5, NLT) "You turned my mourning into dancing; you removed my sackcloth and clothed me with joy, that my heart may sing your praises and not be silent." (Psalms 30:11-12, NIV) "My future is in your hands. Rescue me from those who hunt me down relentlessly. Let your favor shine on your servant. In your unfailing love, rescue me." (Psalms 31:15-16, NLT) Are you hearing God's songs to help you start the day? Every day with God is a beautiful day when you place that day into His caring hands.

One of my favorite scriptures dealing with this subject is found in an Old Testament book that most people never read - the book of Lamentations. (The title gives you a clue as to why it is not a book of favorite reading.) But look at these words of optimistic encouragement to begin each day: "Because of the LORD's great love we are not consumed, for his compassions never fail. They are new every morning; great is your faithfulness." (Lamentations 3:22–23, NIV) Herein is a truth to start each day. God sees every day with great optimism for your life. He forgets the past every morning and His great compassions and faithfulness never fail. Maybe you should start singing with Gordon, "Oh 'God', what a beautiful morning..."

A Beautiful Life

Springtime in the South is a sight to behold. The indescribable brilliance of an Azalea plant in bloom ignites the eye with a vision that almost takes your breath away. The colors are direct from the heart and imagination of God. Almost every year my wife and I travel to Bellingrath Gardens in Mobile Alabama to see the azaleas in bloom. They claim to have several million varieties of azalea plants and I believe it. The trick each year, is to arrive when the blooms are at their peak. If you're early, all you see is a rather ugly green leafed bush. If you arrive too late, you see the leftovers of a color party you missed with dead discolored pedals piled everywhere. But when you arrive right on time, you are swept away to Dorothy's Oz, and dance with her along the yellow brick road with its pathways of color.

I think our lives in many ways mimic an azalea plant. We get planted on this earth and spend our lives sprouting branches in every direction stretching to reach our potential. But mostly, we're just unproductive green bushes. People we encounter in our lives don't see much value in us, because they look just like we do. In fact, everywhere where we look, are green wiry bushes, brushing against each other, as the breezes of life blow against us.

Then we discover the truth about God and invite Jesus into our bland unshapely lives. And, "Viola!" we start blooming with His brilliance, as His life courses through ours. Before you know it, we have shape, beauty and purpose in life. The blooms that everyone sees are His life bursting through our drab existence. Then suddenly, others begin to spout into color, as they too invite Christ into their lives, and the eternal life in Christ becomes visible. The contagious personality of Christ draws our family, friends and neighbors to His love and acceptance, and one by one, the mundane lives of hopeless and tired people become what they always wanted life to be – beautiful.

Does all this sound too fanciful to believe? It's not. God loves you and sees your needs. He sent His Son to change your life. All you need to do is trust Him and turn your life over to Him. He is the master husbandman and keeper of our garden. He wants to transform your life. The bible says, "… to bestow on them a crown of beauty instead of ashes, the oil of joy instead of mourning, and a garment of praise instead of a spirit of despair. They will be called oaks (my word=azaleas) of righteousness, a planting of the LORD for the display of his splendor." (Isaiah 61:3, NIV)

Abortion and the Constitution

Have you read the First Amendment to the United States Constitution lately? Just in case you haven't, here it is: "Congress shall make no law respecting an establishment of religion, or prohibiting the free exercise thereof; or abridging the freedom of speech, or of the press; or the right of the people peaceably to assemble, and to petition the Government for a redress of grievances." Any law in direct conflict with the tenants of faith and morals of the church are unconstitutional. They would be a direct attack on Christianity that is forbidden by the United States Constitution. "Congress shall make no law respecting an establishment of religion, or <u>prohibiting the free exercise thereof…</u>"

Our founding fathers pledged their lives, fortunes and sacred honor to insure that unjust laws would not be enforced on the people of the United States. The preachers of that day stood in the pulpits and declared that any law, by the then dictator King George, must not be obeyed, when those laws stood in direct conflict with the Word of God. The mandates of laws concerning the life of the unborn are not only unconstitutional, they fly in the face of God and His Law that says, "You shall not murder." (Exodus 20:13, NIV)

When Adolph Hitler came to power, he made plans for the destruction of Judaism and Christianity. He cloaked his devious plans by professing to be a Christian. He encouraged his closest advisers to maintain an air of Christianity until the final trap was sprung. Hitler set a mandate to ban all Jews from participation and offices in any Christian organization. The Christian church, gulped, and followed the mandate. It wasn't long before the smoke began to bellow from the concentration camps and both Jews and Christians were murdered together. The problem stemmed in part from the lazy fearful Christian Church that refused to stand up to ungodly mandates by the ungodly national leaders. Some would say, this is not Germany, and Hitler is not in charge. I say, history repeats itself. We must stand or we will fall. Our founding father, Benjamin Franklin, said it this way. "We must, indeed, all hang together, or assuredly we shall all hang separately..."

We cannot and must not allow any attack by the unjust on Christianity to continue. The next edict may be that Christian doctors MUST murder the unborn or face fines and imprisonment. Then laws will be passed that pastors will not be able to publicly speak of sin and its consequences. It's a very slippery slope.

Accepted by God

Have you ever been excluded or felt excluded by someone? A lifetime of exclusion, or perceived exclusion, can cause you to live life believing that you are not up to the level of other people. When I was a boy my dad gave me a bit of advice about life. He said, "Don't ever feel that other people are better than you. Every man puts his pants on one leg at a time." Simple, yet profound. According to my dad everyone is on an equal playing field in this world.

We are, in many ways, products of our environment. We use speech that gives away where we are from. "Who dat say da gonna beat dem Saints?" is a perfect example of speech used by New Orleans Saints football fans. The way we dress… our manners etc… all tell about who we are. Now, your environment growing up may not have been the best. Your parents may have been divorced or died. You may have been reared in a poor home or a home without love. Maybe you were abused. Maybe you lived a less than stellar life and have lots of skeletons in your closet. All these circumstances have hammered you down and left you feeling inadequate. If that's you, I have great news! Jesus came to set you free!

God was looking for you before He created the world. "For he chose us in him before the creation of the world to be holy and blameless in his sight. In love…" (Ephesians 1:4, NIV) The key word here is "chose." God was looking for someone to love and He chose you. You may think you are not much in this world, but God knows you are someone very special. He even sent His Son to invite you to live in His neighborhood. A place where everyone is special. A place where goodness flows. A place where you can prosper all the days of your life and throughout all eternity. That place is the family of God. You are wanted and accepted there. When you accept the invitation of Jesus to join His family, everything changes for you. You become a child of the King of Kings. You have royal blood flowing through you. That royal blood is the blood of Jesus, shed at Calvary, just for you. Stop seeing yourself as rejected and start seeing yourself as God sees you. "To the praise of the glory of His grace, by which He made us (you) accepted in the Beloved (His Family)." (Ephesians 1:6, NKJ)

America and Spiritual Freedom

Most of the world is not free. It is held in bondage by dictators and tyrants of every imaginable breed. History testifies that the majority of humanity has suffered and been used as slave-pawns by a few elites, since Adam and Eve were ushered from the Garden of Eden. The maternal twins, sin and death, entered the world when Adam ate of the forbidden fruit and have grown like cancer to infect every child born of woman. What started as simple disobedience has morphed into mass murder, abuse, slavery, immorality and hatred of every variety.

In the course of time, under the direction of God, a group of men and women believed that the cruelty they saw in the world, was in direct opposition to truth found in the scriptures. They penned a document that recognized that God created men with certain unalienable rights: Life, Liberty, and the Pursuit of Happiness. They did not confer these rights on people, but declared that these rights were "self evident", and must be recognized. They stated, in the strongest possible language, that governments were only valid when the people gave the government the privilege of governing over them. This government was not for the cruel elite, so they could lord over the common man, but was to insure that everyone was treated equally. The government could not determine who was to be elite and who was relegated to the bottom of the economic ladder. The status in life was to be determined by each individual. The government was to make sure no one interfered with the process. And with those thoughts in mind, The United States of America was born upon the earth July 4, 1776.

Never before or since have men enjoyed such freedom. That freedom was carved out, and is sustained by the bearers of the flag of freedom. Every American must stand watch to insure that a free America never fails, because if it does, the world will once again fall under the strong hand of the oppressors. President Ronald Reagan called America, "A shining city on a hill." This light must not dim or fail to shine for the entire world to see. The Statue of Liberty hails these words on her base and her lips: *Give me your tired, your poor, Your huddled masses yearning to breathe free, The wretched refuse of your teeming shore. Send these, the homeless, tempest-tossed, to me: I lift my lamp beside the golden door.*

As you celebrate each Forth of July, remember to thank God for establishing this land of the free. Freedom is a gift from God. Jesus even declared that He came to set captives free. "So if the Son sets you free, you will be free indeed." (John 8:36, NIV)

Ancient Deities in Modern Times

The Lenten season is here in New Orleans and many people will be following the ancient tradition of giving up something for the next 40 days. No candy. No alcoholic beverages. No movies. And no meat, which makes the cows happy, and the local fish try to swim up river, like a salmon, to save their lives.

But you know what I don't get? I don't get the New Orleans' Mardi Gras. It seems odd to me that Mardi Gras gives permission to go wild the day before Lent begins. Maybe we need a new Mardi Gras song to the tune of "Pants on the Ground" (If you don't know this one, go to You Tube.) The lyrics would be something like "Sin all around. Sin all around. Looking like a fool with your sin all around." People go to parades with names of ancient evil deities, raise their hands in a mock praise, and yell for the masked people to throw them something. Maybe I'm the only one, but doesn't that seem weird, and just the opposite of what Christians ought to be doing?

Then the day after Mardi Gras people go to church, and return with ashes on their head, reminding them that they are going to die and go back to the dust of the earth one day. What if God showed up on Mardi Gras and you were caught raising your hands to Bacchus – the god of drunkenness, or Endymion – the god of sexuality, or Pegasus – the winged horse deity?

Christians are to give up things not only for Lent, but some things ought to be avoided all the time. Look at what God's Word says about Mardi Gras type behavior: "Because we belong to the day, we must live decent lives for all to see. Don't participate in the darkness of wild parties and drunkenness, or in sexual promiscuity and immoral living, or in quarreling and jealousy. Instead, clothe yourself with the presence of the Lord Jesus Christ. And don't let yourself think about ways to indulge your evil desires." (Romans 13:13-14, NLT)

I'm all for Lent, but as for me and my house, we'll avoid Mardi Gras. How about you?

Awe Filled Church

How do you feel when you leave church services on Sundays? Beat up? Disappointed? Glad its over? Joyful? Awe filled? Hate to leave? I'm sure all of us would say we've experienced a host of emotions when leaving church services. Perhaps the worst thing we feel is "nothing."

When you read the New Testament you find the early church experienced joy and awe even in the midst of the hardships they suffered. "And the disciples were filled with joy and with the Holy Spirit." (Acts 13:52, NIV) "With great power the apostles continued to testify to the resurrection of the Lord Jesus. And God's grace was so powerfully at work in them all." (Acts 4:33, NIV) What did they know that we have forgotten, or worst have never experienced?

I believe what kept them excited was the excitement. There were miracles. Healings. Hosts of people were coming to Christ. Danger. But the greatest excitement was the understanding that they were part of an awesome move of God. Does that describe your religious experience? Probably not! The worst thing the church has done is to showcase respectability, fancy buildings, seminary-trained sermons and the ability to entertain ourselves for an hour or so each week. The church was designed to reach out to the hurting of the world and offer them hope. The last thing Jesus said to the early church was a commission to get out and get going. "Therefore go and make disciples of all nations…" (Matthew 28:19, NIV) Today we "go" to church instead of "going" to the world.

We have traded the joy and excitement of Christianity for institutional traditions that fail to energize us. This week take a risk and tell someone about Jesus. You'll stop singing B.B. Kings, "The thrill is gone" and start shouting James Brown's, "I feel good!" You might even fire up your pastor for a change.

"Therefore go and make disciples of all nations, baptizing them in the name of the Father and of the Son and of the Holy Spirit, and teaching them to obey everything I have commanded you. And surely I am with you always, to the very end of the age." (Matthew 28:19–20 NIV)

Baptism of the Holy Spirit

Have you ever bought something and when you got it home found out that it didn't work as advertised? On rare occasions, you might buy an item and find that it does more than you thought. Several years ago I bought a new car with as many bells and whistles as I could afford. After driving the car for a few days I noticed a strange bump on the backside of the steering wheel right where my hand rested on the wheel. My fingers would touch it as they closed around the wheel. I noticed that, on occasions, the radio station would change without my touching the radio dials. I was ready to bring the car back to the dealer to get the radio fixed, when I finally realized the strange bump was actually a hidden radio switch that changed the pre-set stations. To my great surprise I found a similar switch on the other side of the steering wheel which controlled the volume. Who knew? I had looked in the manual and there was no indication these switches existed. Even the salesman didn't know about it.

Christianity is like that car. It has benefits that you don't even know about. In the book of Acts chapter 19 there is an account of what I'm referring to. The Apostle Paul came upon a few new disciples and asked them if they had received the Holy Spirit since they believed. They answered, "No, we have not even heard that there is a Holy Spirit." (Acts 19:2, NIV) Paul asked them what baptism they had received and they replied, "John's baptism." Paul explained that John's baptism was about repentance but that they needed another Baptism into Jesus. They then received the better baptism in the name of the Lord Jesus. "When Paul placed his hands on them, the Holy Spirit came on them, and they spoke in tongues and prophesied." (Acts 19:6, NIV) They didn't know about the buttons on the other side of the wheel, so-to-speak. Are you a Believer but have never received the Baptism of the Holy Spirit? Unlike my car, this is written in God's instruction manual, the bible.

There is more to Christianity that you may have thought. We are forgiven and redeemed by faith in Jesus. But we are empowered by the Holy Spirit to change the world. Jesus said this right before He left earth and went into heaven: "Do not leave Jerusalem, but wait for the gift my Father promised, which you have heard me speak about. For John baptized with water, but in a few days you will be baptized with the Holy Spirit." (Acts 1:4-5, NIV) Why not study this for yourself and see what you may be missing.

Be Thankful

Just one more holiday and we can have peace on earth once again. The holiday season will be over for another year. Yet we seem determined to look forward to the next big event on the calendar, hoping it will bring the fun and excitement we are searching for in life. But when we get there, the expectation is dimmed by the reality. The truth is that everything in life is never what we anticipate it will be. The most famous prognosticator of this truism is the biblical wise man, Solomon. He put it this way: "'Meaningless! Meaningless!' says the Teacher. 'Utterly meaningless! Everything is meaningless.'" (Ecclesiastes 1:2, NIV) Now that's a negative attitude about the future. Solomon tried everything under the sun to find happiness and discovered the pleasures, wealth, and wisdom of the world never satisfy. He finally concluded that the only lasting joy is found in knowing God and following His plans for your life.

If last year has left you feeling like everything is hopeless, then make up your mind to spend next year looking to God and discovering a fresh relationship with Him. The joy of life is the unseen reality of interacting with the Living God. God is searching for those who will let Him love them. That may seem strange since, so often, we are told to love God. But He wants you to receive His love. He is always reaching out with words and acts of love to those who are willing to receive Him. How do you receive His love? You respond to His goodness with words of thanks and appreciation. Thank Him for His presence in your life, as well as the presents He gives to you. The ability to see and hear. The love of family. A home to live in. A child to love. Your health. The sun. The rain. All these and more are gifts from God. But the greatest gift of all is eternal life that is presented to you through God's only Son – Jesus. Don't look for satisfaction in all the wrong places. Look to God next year and I promise you the happiest New Year you will every have.

Bible and School

Yikes! It's back to school again. I hated school from the first day my mother deserted me in a room full of crying children until the day I took my final exam in college. I shed an ocean of tears, sweat and blood getting my education. The tears were caused by self-pity because I had to go through the learning process. The sweat was trying to understand all that "useless" information found in mountains of books. The blood was from the discipline I endured at school and at home. (Yes, they used to beat you into submission back in the day.) But I survived it all and discovered the education I hated was the key to unlock the doors of success in America. I hated the process but I loved the results.

Then one day I discovered that with all my education, I was missing a vital element, and without that missing link I would die. I was stunned to learn, with my cranium filled with reading, 'riting, and 'rithmetic, I did not know anything about the most important subject in life. A very wise and "fully" educated man asked me a question that I was unable to answer. He asked me what would happen to me when I died? I was slack-jawed and unable to respond, other than to babble a few religious things I had picked up along the way. I had no clue what would happen to me when I died.

He asked if he could show me a few things in the bible. The bible was never in any curriculum I endured, so I said sure. What I discovered that day changed my life. No, it more than changed - it gave me life. I found myself ushered back into school but this time I loved it. No, I craved it. Every page was a fountain of truth I never knew. This ancient book was filled with truths that changed my life, my marriage and every aspect of my search for happiness. The one passage in scripture that turned me around when I read it for the first time states: "But seek ye first the kingdom of God, and his righteousness; and all these things shall be added unto you." (Matthew 6:33, KJV) The missing link was seeking God first! When I learned to do that everything changed. I'm still in school and will be until graduation day. That's the day I leave planet earth and stand before the Savior of the world – Jesus the Christ.   How about you? What's first priority on your list of life?

Black Robe Regiment

The election is over and the results are known. At the time I am writing this article the election has not occurred. The political forecasters of elections predict this election will be a major shift in the profile of America. The majority of officials elected may be Republican who will gain control of the House and the Senate shifting control away from the Democrats. This is good or bad depending on your political persuasion. But, be fully aware that predictions of elections are often wrong. Remember Truman and Dewey? The headlines on the day after the election in broad print declared Dewey the new president. However, Truman had won.

But what do you do now? I believe the pulpits of America have a responsibility to put on their black robes and proclaim the truth to their congregations. I hope they do so. I have. My congregation was stunned to see me in a black robe as I preached of my responsibility to join the Black Robe Regiment of 1776 and stand against corruption in America.

Now it's time for you to do your part. You begin by educating yourself about the issues of the day and know how the elected officials are speaking and voting on vital issues. Then you make sure they know how you feel about the way they are voting. Hold their feet to the fire! They are there to serve you and if they do a bad, illegal or immoral job, do all in your power to usher them out of office.

In 1933 an unknown man was elected to office in Germany and by the end of 1945 an estimated 60 to 70 million people were dead around the world because of that man. His name was Adolph Hitler. A German pastor, Martin Niemoller was arrested by the Gestapo in 1937. He wrote a famous poem about that:

"They came first for the Communists,
and I didn't speak up because I wasn't a Communist.
Then they came for the Jews,
and I didn't speak up because I wasn't a Jew.
Then they came for the trade unionists,
and I didn't speak up because I wasn't a trade unionist.
Then they came for the Catholics,

and I didn't speak up because I was a Protestant.
Then they came for me,
and by that time no one was left to speak up."

Don't fail to use your first amendment right of free speech and "speak up" while you still can.

Blessings

There's a lot to be thankful for as citizens of this great nation. Sure, we have issues and disappointments, but compared to most of the world, we live in Paradise. There was a bumper snicker a long time ago that said, "Stop criticizing the farmers with your mouth full." That says a lot about our unthankful attitude at times. We are blessed beyond measure in America, and it's fitting that we have at lease one day a year when we give thanks to God for all that He has done to enhance our lives.

There is an interesting paradox in the book of Hosea. The people of Israel kept turning away from God and worshiping idols made with their hands. They bowed down to everything but to God who was caring for them. God was distressed because the more He did for them and the more He blessed them, the faster they walked in the other direction. Listen to the heart of God, "I led them with cords of human kindness, with ties of love. To them I was like one who lifts a little child to the cheek, and I bent down to feed them." (Hosea 11:4, NIV) God said, I taught them to walk, I fed them and I called them to come to me. "But the more they were called, the more they went away from me." (Hosea 11:2, NIV)

Does any of this sound like America? We are prosperous beyond measure. We have freedom that other nations can only imagine. The blessings of God are a canopy that shades us from much harm. Why then do we drive Him out of our government, schools, businesses and families?

Israel suffered much because they refused to have a thankful heart and recognize who was their divine benefactor. Let's pray that America turns back to God so that we don't experience the famine and blight others suffered because they ran away from Him. Father loves us, and it's His heart's desire that we return to His loving arms.

Broken People

I carefully pulled my car off Interstate 10 in New Orleans East near Lake Pontchartrain looking for a swampy area where the cattails were growing near the side of the road. No, my car had not broken down. I was on my way home from my office in New Orleans where I had spent the day with my ten-year-old daughter enjoying a daughter-day-at-the-office. She was sitting next to me as we were driving home and said, "Dad, would you get me one of those cattails?" I agreed and dodged a few cars as I pulled next to a field of the brown corn-dogs-on-a-stick-looking reeds. I stepped out of my car and placed my black wing tip shoes in the damp soggy marsh hoping to get a reed before a gator got my leg. I picked out a nice one only to have the tender reed bend in half in my grip. I had to discard a few broken cattails before I gathered a tall bouquet for my baby girl. She was overjoyed at the treasure I handed her. Neither my daughter nor I have forgotten that memorable day.

Broken cattails are not worth taking home when they are bent in two. Who would want to decorate their house with them? They are only worth discarding. Those who like these plants only want those with strong stems that will grace a vase and proudly stand up for all to see. I guess by now you are wondering what cattails have to do with Christianity. They have a lot when you read a verse of scripture from the prophet Isaiah that was repeated in the New Testament. "He will not crush the weakest reed or put out a flickering candle. He will bring justice to all who have been wronged." (Isaiah 42:3, NLT)

Have you ever felt like a broken cattail reed that is bent over by the crippling weight of life? Maybe your spouse has deserted you. Maybe you have done something that you feel God can never forgive. Maybe you got fired from your job. Maybe you're just bent over in the marsh of life. No one seems to care about you. "He will not crush the weakest reed," is a promise of hope from God our Father. He sees you and has great compassion for you. He will tenderly reach out and support you until you regain your strength. Others may step on you as they look for better fields to harvest, but God will not pass you by. That's a promise He will never break. Perk up. God loves to fix broken people. Oh, and if you have an opportunity, take a child on a holiday. You may make an unforgettable memory.

Choosing to Avoid Evil

"Carnival Time" is the "unofficial" official song by Al Johnson that is sung ad infinitum during the Mardi Gras season. The lyrics in part are, "The green room is smoking, and the plaza burning down, throw my baby out the window, let those joints burn down. All because it's Carnival Time, wooooooohhh, it's Carnival Time... Oh well it's Carnival Time and everybody's having fun!" Now that's a message I need to hear! We have two places on fire, and we're going to throw someone out the window and let them burn down. And the reason is because it's Carnival Time and everybody's having fun. Well, not everyone is having fun. I'm not.

Okay, I know I'm stuck in the primeval mud, but I can't help myself. I hate Carnival Time! The streets are blocked and I'm forced to try and find alternate routes to get somewhere. There is debris all over where the citizens have thrown broken beads and stuff, and left them for someone else to clean up. Morals seem to have regressed to the time when Moses came down from a meeting with God and found the people in a drunken revelry worshiping a golden calf. This is not a fun time and I certainly would not bring my children or grandchildren to a place where God is forgotten and evil is personified as "fun."

Will you go to hell for going to the Mardi Gras? The answer is no. You go to hell for a much more serious offense: not believing that Jesus is your Lord and Savior. However, you will be experiencing an event that is devoid of God and honors evil. That seems to me to be a place to avoid and not visit. The scriptures admonish us to avoid every appearance of evil. We are to be children of light, not of darkness. We are to honor God with our lives, not the devil's schemes and devises. The bible asks the question, "What will you be doing when Jesus returns to earth?" I don't think it's a good idea to be at the Mardi Gras, but hey that's just me. By the way, just so you don't think I'm a complete prude, I actually like the song. The music is catchy and makes you want to sing along. It's the lyrics and message I don't like.

Christmas and Memories

Barbra Streisand and Robert Redford, a million years ago in 1973, brought a blockbuster movie and song to the world titled "The Way We Were." The lilting lyrics and captivating voice of Streisand as she sang, "Mem'ries, light the corners of my mind, misty water-colored memories, of the way we were…" put us in a melancholy mood each time we heard it played. Memories are a mysterious part of our lives. A faint fragrance, an old tattered picture, a song etched in our minds or a thought out of nowhere, sets off an avalanche of memories in our minds.

Perhaps no time of the year stimulates our memories more than the Christmas season. We remember those who are no longer with us. Mom and Dad. A child. A friend. A spouse. Those memories bring smiles to our hearts and tears to our eyes. Either way, we each deal with our memories of those we can no longer physically touch. This is why for many people Christmas is not very merry but a time when depression pierces their lives and robs them of the joy of the season.

The first Christmas long ago was unveiled with a song. A choir of angels serenaded the shepherds with, "Glory to God in the highest heaven, and on earth peace to those on whom his favor rests." (Luke 2:14, NIV) Time has replaced these hopeful lyrics of the shepherds racing to the manger with "Jingle Bells" and "Santa Clause is Coming to Town." No wonder we get pulled down at Christmas.

This Christmas season do yourself a favor. Let your memories be filled with the blessed hope that Jesus brought into the world. He came with the promise that those who are no longer here will be seen again in heaven one day. He came to remind you that you are not alone. He is with you. He came to fill your life with peace. The modern Christmas has become a time of turmoil introduced by, of all things, "Black Friday." Let your mind dwell on the good things God has given you and forget the confusion of the distorted secular Christmas created by the world.

"And now, dear brothers and sisters, one final thing. Fix your thoughts on what is true, and honorable, and right, and pure, and lovely, and admirable. Think about things that are excellent and worthy of praise." (Philippians 4:8, NLT)

Day of Prayer

Thomas Paine on December 23, 1776 wrote, "These are the times that try men's souls. The summer soldier and the sunshine patriot will, in this crisis, shrink from the service of their country; but he that stands by it now, deserves the love and thanks of man and woman."

The fledging United States, a scant five months old, was in a fight for her life. This new America, with the ink of the Declaration of Independence still damp, stood toe to toe with the most powerful nation on earth, fighting for her God-declared liberty. But there was another battle raging on her shores. The division was between those who claimed liberty now and liberty forever against those who swore allegiance to the British crown. The country was split.

Paine wrote of "summer soldiers and sunshine patriots" who were willing to fight for America on sunny days when the skies were blue and nights were warm and the fierce New England winters were not freezing and brutalizing the American army in the open field. Those certainly were the "Times that try men's souls."

Today, 235 plus years later we find America in another war for principles once again. Thank God, the sounds we hear are the blast of words via electronic speakers on TV and at political rallies, and not the belch of cannons and the smoke of muskets aimed to inflict bodily harm. Yet, the passions are just as high as they were in 1776. Our nation is divided and the war of words fills the country with a stench of hatred from sea to shinning sea.

What can we to do to bring peace and unity to America once again? We will do what America has always done in times of crisis. We will pray! Our leaders, from George Washington to virtually every president who has held the highest office in our fair land, have called Americans to pray. The first Thursday in May of every year has been designated as a National Day of Prayer. Prayers will be uttered from every corner of our nation for the well being of our land of liberty. Please take time to pray and ask God to unite us once again around His throne of grace. We have a sacred duty to do so in honor of those who spilled their blood in 1776 for peace and freedom. God promises to hear and heal our land if we pray (2 Chronicles 7:14, NIV) "If my people, who are called by my name, will humble themselves and pray and seek my face and turn from their wicked ways, then will I hear from heaven and will forgive their sin and will heal their land."

Dead in Christ are Alive

"I am the Resurrection!" was Jesus' reply when He was in a conversation about people dying. It interests me that He did not say, "You will be resurrected." Neither did He say, "I will be resurrected." No, His statement was more earth shattering than anything else He could have said. He claimed to be "The Resurrection."

Did you notice the "I am" of His declaration? Does it sound familiar? Here's a clue: Moses at the burning bush. Yep! God declared Himself to be the "I Am" when Moses asked Him who He was. That encounter by Moses began one of the greatest movements of God recorded in the scriptures. Jesus was sending us a message that He was "I Am" and even more. Moses set people free from captivity, but Jesus was about to set people free from death.

Notice, "The Resurrection," declares that there is only one resurrection of life. The dead are raised to life at the end of the age, but is that "The Resurrection?"

No! That's an event that will occur but that's not "The Resurrection." Jesus is "The Resurrection." It's His DNA. Only He can make something that is dead be raised to life. "The Resurrection" is the only source of eternal life. "But because of his great love for us, God, who is rich in mercy, made us alive with Christ even when we were dead in transgressions—it is by grace you have been saved. And God raised us up with Christ and seated us with him in the heavenly realms in Christ Jesus." (Ephesians 2:4-6, NIV) When you receive Jesus by faith as your Savior, you actually receive "The Resurrection." You are immediately raised from the dead and made alive! How awesome is that?

You see friends, Jesus was promising that the resurrection is more than a future event, it is the "I Am" and the "Only Son" by the power of "The Holy Spirit" guaranteeing that those who believe the Gospel of Jesus will never die, but have (present tense) "The Resurrection." Oh, there will be a day when the graves of the earth pop open your mortal body will leap to the sky to meet Jesus in the air and be fashioned anew like Jesus, but as far as God is concerned, you are already "raised with Christ." Think about it for a while and give Him praise.

Depression

James Brown, the ultimate rocker, sang, "I feel good!" in his hit song, "I got you." And all of America began to jump and shout, as they now felt good too. Sometimes all we need to feel better is someone to tell us its okay to feel good. The vast majority of people you know have trouble feeling good. Life has crushed them down and they can't think of any reason in the world to feel good. So they resort to the depression mode. Then in hopes of getting out of depression they: drink, smoke, eat, cry, pop pills, and fight with the nearest person they can find. There must be a better way to feel good?

Actually, long before James Brown said it, the Apostle Paul shouted it to the world. He used different words but the message and the tune was the same. "Rejoice in the Lord always. I will say it again:

Rejoice!" (Philippians 4:4, NIV) But James Brown never told you how you could feel good. He only said that "He" felt good. Paul said that "You" could feel good. Therein lies the difference between humanity's philosophy and God's theology. Philosophy is selfish and cares about itself but God cares about you and how you feel.

Paul gives a foolproof formula to start you feeling good again. First, he says we need to be aware that God is near and that you are not alone. "The Lord is near." (Philippians 4:5, NIV) This is what we need more than anything – The presence of God. If God is near, we know He loves us and He is interested in our lives. Second, he says we need to talk to God and tell Him how we feel and what's going on (See Philippians 4:6-7). Yes, you can dump on God! He understands and you won't hurt His feelings. Don't believe me? Go read the Psalms of David and see how he spoke to God when he was in trouble. Third, Paul says to change what you're thinking about. Stop believing the sky is falling and start believing the blessings of God are falling. "Finally, brothers, whatever is true, whatever is noble, whatever is right, whatever is pure, whatever is lovely, whatever is admirable—if anything is excellent or praiseworthy—think about such things." (Philippians 4:8, NIV) And it wouldn't hurt you to go to iTunes and buy a copy of James Brown's song and start singing, "I feel good!"

Desertion and Despair

What a difference a day can make. Quite often the discouragements of life make us feel that life is void of any hope. I believe the close circle of men Jesus surrounded Himself with, must have felt that way when Jesus died on the cross. They had just witnessed and experienced the most horrible event in history. The Son of God had died on a Roman cross. But more than that, they just lost their best friend. And to add fuel to the fire, they had all just deserted Him when He needed their friendship the most.

The desertion started at the Last Supper when Judas sold Jesus out for a few silver coins. He's a special case, but the others fell into their own self-preservation trap. Peter had boldly declared that he would never desert Jesus and a few hours later he swore he never knew him. One by one they left Jesus standing alone. John, to his credit, was at the cross, but one out of twelve is a poor representation of the "holy" apostles. I can only imagine the way they must have felt. Peter finally said what was in his heart. "I'm going fishing." And he did. And the others went with him.

So despair won out over faith. "Have you caught any fish?" a supposed stranger shouted across the water to them as they sat with empty nets and hearts. "Nope!" was the downtrodden reply. They failed at friendship. They failed at apostleship. They went back to what they knew before Jesus called them, and they were failing at fishing too. "Throw you net on the other side of the boat." The stranger shouted through their glum dispositions. They did, and hauled in a net breaking load of fish. Peter suddenly realized the stranger was Jesus and shouted with an old familiar excitement that only Jesus could create in him, "It's the Lord!" He left his despair in the boat as he jumped into the water and arrived on shore where Jesus was fixing a fried fish breakfast for His "A" team. The rest paddled to the banks right behind Peter. Their spirits were lifted, they reengaged into the work of the Kingdom, and their journey continued. Before they knew it, they were harvesting thousands of fish-souls into the Kingdom of God.

So how are you doing? Are you catching anything? Follow Jesus' advice. Forget yesterday's failures.

And try something new. Let your net of life down on the other side and get ready for a fresh net breaking harvest in your life. Who knows? You might even shout like Peter, "It's the Lord!"

Directions

The Romans had captured most of the known world by the time Jesus was born. They brought their culture, laws and ingenuity wherever they went. We have a saying that declares, "All roads lead to Rome." The reason we say that is because the Romans were the interstate builders of their day. In fact, if you laid out just the paved roads they built across America, they would create 17 Interstate highways from the east to the west coast. That does not take into account the additional 200,000 miles of dirt roads they constructed.

When the Romans wanted to get somewhere they had superhighways to get there. One interesting aspect of those paved roads was that every mile had a milepost that indicated where you were on any particular road so you would never get lost. It was their version of a GPS system. I guess even the Romans hated to ask for directions when they got lost.

We have managed to make American society a place where you always know where you are. Google is the ultimate tool you can use to ask to find the nearest Starbucks or gas station, depending on which needs filling – you or your car.

But how about when you need spiritual directions? That's a bit more difficult a road for us to travel. However, if you know how to read the signs, you can find help anytime. For example, God says when you are tempted to do evil He will provide a way of escape. He says you can tell where He is at any time by just looking at the beauty of the Universe He created.

God promises to be a friend that sticks closer than a brother. Jesus said when you feed someone, visit a sick person or even offer friendship to someone in jail, you are actually doing those things to Him. You see, when you know how to read the spiritual milestones, you'll find that God is everywhere that you are. So in truth you are never really lost. "You go before me and follow me. You place your hand of blessing on my head. Such knowledge is too wonderful for me, too great for me to understand! I can never escape from your Spirit! I can never get away from your presence!" (Psalms 139:5-7, NLT)

The next time you feel spiritually lost, stop and ask Him for directions. He is right beside you.

DNA and Decisions

Sometimes I hate to make decisions. I always have the problem of trying to decide what is God's will and what is mine. I'm of the opinion that God will be interested in the decision process of any situation if we will ask Him to be involved. I know Believers who have the opinion that God does not take part in any of our decisions. Other Believers believe that God is only interested in "major" decisions. And then there are Believers, like me, who believe God wants to be part of every decision from the color of the clothes you wear to the major issues such as marriage and ministry.

So who's right? I am of course! But the reason I believe I'm right is based on the scriptures. God has been interested in you since before you were born. He was so interested in details that He chose your unique DNA. "You made all the delicate, inner parts of my body and knit me together in my mother's womb.

Thank you for making me so wonderfully complex! Your workmanship is marvelous—how well I know it." (Psalms 139:13-14, NLT) I think this is proof that God is interested in little things. And what about your entire life span? He is watching over you and taking a direct interest in your changes in life so much so that he counts the hairs on your head. "And the very hairs on your head are all numbered." (Matthew 10:30, NLT) Then there's the issue of wisdom to make right decisions. "If you need wisdom, ask our generous God, and he will give it to you. He will not rebuke you for asking." (James 1:5, NLT) I could go on and on about the things that God is interested in concerning you but I think I've made my case. God has always cared about you and wants to be involved in every aspect of your life.

Try asking God about little things and get accustomed to hearing His voice and seeing the proof of His involvement. Start with parking places at Walmart and work your way up to what His eternal purpose is for your life. You will be pleasantly surprised at how many great parking places you find and how much peace you have about life's decisions because of the wisdom of God directing your steps. This commentary is a result of asking God what He wanted to say to you today. I started with a blank mind (don't laugh) and a blank computer screen. I had an idea and it felt like God was speaking to me and here are the results. If you don't like this article blame God. As for me, I like it.

Doldrums and Boredoms

The long days of the summer doldrums are here in full force. It's hot everywhere. There are no new movies to go see. TV is rerun city. Even the news programs are in rerun mode. (How can today's news be a rerun?) I think the department stores are rerunning last year's everything-must-go-sale, when they didn't sell everything. Even Church attendance is down. Imagine that!

So what do you do in the doldrums of life when even boredom is ho-hum? You could read the book of Numbers in the bible. That's where most people start presuming the bible is a very boring book. I have a better idea. How about reading the book of Acts. Even its name gives you a hint that something big was going on. Acts! This book has everything. The Holy

Spirit showed up in a hurricane of wind and fire and changed the course of history. The disciples got so fired up that the locals who came to see what all the noise was about thought they were drunk. Peter started preaching on the street corner about Jesus and 3,000 people gave their lives to God. How's that for excitement?

Acts goes on with one electrifying event after another. A lame man gets healed and walks for the first time in his life. A husband and wife team drops dead in church when they lied about how much they gave to the church. (Be afraid. Be very afraid.) A man who was on his way to arrest some of the new saints in the church gets knocked off the horse he was riding and saw the resurrected Jesus. There are witches. Shipwrecks. Miracles everywhere.

So what about you? If you are in the doldrums get into Acts instead. Read it and then do it. Don't you think God wants you to be busy in His Kingdom instead of sitting around waiting for the cool breezes of fall to kick in? Here's a sample from Acts that got everyone energized:

> "Then Peter said, 'Silver or gold I do not have, but what I do have I give you. In the name of

Jesus Christ of Nazareth, walk.' Taking him by the right hand, he helped him up, and instantly the man's feet and ankles became strong. He jumped to his feet and began to walk. Then he went with them into the temple courts, walking and jumping, and praising God." (Acts 3:6-8, NIV)

How about that? Go ahead and keep reading, you will love it.

Doors of Direction

"How many times do I have to tell you to close the door?!" my mother used to say. Doors are items that we leave open, slam shut, lock, bolt and use to keep us safe. Doors in the scriptures are used by God to help direct our lives. He can open doors or shut them. When God opens a door, no one can shut it. And when he shuts a door, no one can open it. "I know your deeds. See, I have placed before you an open door that no one can shut. I know that you have little strength, yet you have kept my word and have not denied my name." (Revelation 3:8, NIV) The bumps and bruises we get are often the result of banging our heads on doors that God has shut.

God wants the best for you and He guides the very steps that you take. He is very much like a parent who holds the hand of a child to keep them from running into the street. "The LORD makes firm the steps of the one who delights in him; though he may stumble, he will not fall, for the LORD upholds him with his hand." (Psalms 37:23-24, NIV) Your life is much safer when you look for those open doors He has placed before you.

There is only one door that God will allow you to open by yourself. It's not the door to riches, wisdom or fame. It's the door to your heart. God gives you the same respect with doors that He requires of you. He won't force open the door to your heart. "Here I am! I stand at the door and knock. If anyone hears my voice and opens the door, I will come in and eat with that person, and they with me." (Revelation 3:20, NIV) The imagery spoken of here is of God coming to your house and sitting down to a meal with you. Wouldn't it be great to tell everyone you know that God shares His time with you? God does even better than sharing a meal with you; He brings the food and cooks the meal. "You serve me a six-course dinner right in front of my enemies." (Psalms 23:5, MSG) He wants your enemies to know that you are one of His favorites. Your enemies will be a bit more careful of messing with you when they learn who your new best friend is. Let Jesus in and "close the door" on your enemies.

Easter

Easter is almost here. The good news is that most of the party animals and profiteers lay low during this time of the year. They are pretty much frightened off by concepts like the crucifixion, Holy Week, resurrection and forgiveness of sins. There are no parades to speak of. The Easter Parade is pretty much a thing of the past. Colored eggs have a hard time competing with the kid's iPads and other electronic gadgets. The only industry that seems to have remained constant is the candy people. And I thank God for that. After all, who can resist biting off the ears of a chocolate bunny? (I know. I have my faults.)

But with the world leaving Christianity alone, we can do whatever we want with no interference. We can call a holy fast during Holy Week and focus on God for a change. We can light candles for a candlelight service, where we silently reflect on what God has done for us by sending His Son to die for our sins. We can watch old movies like "The Robe" and "The Ten Commandments," and the new one, "The

Passion" by Mel Gibson. (Please ignore the fact that Gibson is a flawed personality. After all, God spoke through a donkey in the bible.)

All in all, Easter is the best holiday of the year. It falls on a Sunday every year, so it's a holiday for most everyone without the government declaring it a holiday. During Christmas everyone is thinking about presents under the tree, but at Easter we get to think about the Lamb of God on The Tree. At Thanksgiving we eat turkey and dressings, but at Easter we eat unleavened bread and drink wine to remember Christ's wounded body and shed blood. For New Years, we resolve to do better, but for Easter we resolve to never forget what God did for us through the death, burial and resurrection of Jesus.

The bible says that Jesus will return for all Believers in the Eastern sky. I'm hoping He comes on Easter Sunday. Wouldn't it be cool to get up early Easter Sunday morning before the sun rises and look expectantly to the East for His return? Who knows, you might be the first to get a glimpse of the Resurrected Christ returning on Easter Sunday morning. Don't forget to go to church services on Easter Sunday.

Easter Bunny Prayer

"Dear Easter Bunny, thank you for sending Jesus for us," prayed my four-year-old granddaughter. After her mother got up off the floor, where she fell from laughter, she explained the theologically correct way to pray at Easter to her daughter.

However, the Easter season is over and the Christian life is moving on to the next event. But maybe we should not move on too fast. Jesus completed His part of the Easter message on the cross, in the grave and through the resurrection. But is that all there is to do after Easter? Jesus actually saved His best action sermon until right before He left planet Earth and ascended into heaven. He had His team of disciples surrounding Him and He said, "All authority in heaven and on earth has been given to me. Therefore go and make disciples of all nations, baptizing them in the name of the Father and of the Son and of the Holy Spirit, and teaching them to obey everything I have commanded you. And surely I am with you always, to the very end of the age." (Matthew 28:18-20, NIV)

Jesus was declaring that He had done what He came to do, and that the next job was now up to us. If you will excuse the Easter Bunny analogy, it was time for the small band of Believers to start multiplying. He assured them the authority He had was now passed on to them and ultimately to us. "YOU go and make disciples and YOU teach them and YOU watch over them. I'll be with YOU until the end, but it's YOUR turn to get the job of spreading the Good News done." (Matthew 28:18-20, My Version)

You see, what Jesus did was make sure the whole world had every opportunity to trade mortal life for eternal life. Those who believe on what Jesus did that first Easter will receive eternal life. The only way the people of the world can make that eternal life trade is for us to tell them what Easter is all about. Our job is to duplicate what Jesus did by sharing the Good News, and to make sure all the children understand the difference between the Easter Bunny and the Easter Savior.

End of Time

Two Cajuns were standing by the side of the road holding up a sign that said, "Turn around. The end is near." A motorist who was driving past them, rolled down his window and shouted, "You religious fanatics need to get a life!" as he blew by. A few seconds later there was the screech of tires, and the loud sound of a crashing car. One of the Cajuns said, "Maybe we should have just written 'Bridge Out' on the sign." Yep, that's the way things go sometimes. We get too enamored with long explanations about events instead of getting to the point.

The end is near! Well, at least nearer than yesterday. A large portion of the population of the world is enamored about the topic of the end of the world. I've lived through several end time scares where people sold their houses and moved to the mountains thinking they would be safe as the world came to an end. They were wrong! Some more recent prognosticators of the end of the world believed it would happen in December of 2012. This time it was based on the Mayan calendar that happened to stop in the year 2012. I actually think the Mayans did a good job of creating a calendar that went that far. What does the bible say about the end of the world? Jesus said the end would come like a thief in the night (see 2 Peter 3:10). In other words when you least expect it to happen – it will. He also said He didn't know when it would end, only the Father knew. Now if Jesus didn't know, what are the chances the Mayans knew?

Maybe we need a sign that says, "Your end is near." That's a more relevant subject to discuss. What's going to happen to you when you end? The bible is covered with information about your end and encourages you to obtain eternal life before it happens. It makes no difference if your life ends with the whole world or your life ends by yourself. Either way – your life in this world will have ended. The only way to survive the end is to have eternal life. That way you will never die. The only way to obtain eternal life is to place your life in the hands of Jesus. "Jesus said to her, 'I am the resurrection and the life. The one who believes in me will live, even though they die.'" (John 11:25, NIV) Now that's a great sign to hold up for everyone to see, just in case the bridge ahead is out.

End Times

What's next? It seems that events, way too big to comprehend, are happening in our world. The Middle East is overthrowing governments. Cataclysmic events, the proportions we rarely read about much less experience, are occurring throughout the world. When I saw the rush of the Tsunami waters in Japan, I remembered Katrina's devastation in my hometown. The threat from the nuclear reactors melting down in Japan gives me flash backs of 1945 when two atomic bombs obliterated Hiroshima and Nagasaki. Who would have thought the people of Japan would have to face nuclear radiation again?

The evidence tells me that all eternity is experiencing trauma. My spiritual Richter scale needle is scratching back and forth indicating that something deep in the Kingdom of God is going on. The shaking began when Jesus died on Calvary's Cross as He cried out and gave up His Spirit. Darkness covered the earth, earthquakes occurred, graves opened and some of the dead were temporarily restored to life. The Temple veil was torn in two from top to bottom and fear entered the hearts of men as they wondered what would become of them. Can you feel the tremors?

One day Jesus will return to earth and there will be no safe place for people to hide. They will run to the mountains, leaving everything behind. They will cry out for mercy, but none will be found. The first time Jesus came to earth He came meek and mild. But the next time He comes He will come in great power. What will happen to you at His second coming? When the sound of His coming is heard around the world it will be too late to do anything to help yourself. Turn to Him today while there is still time. Ask Him to enter your life and make you alive in Christ, so that when He returns, He will gather you to Himself before the rod of the judgment strikes the earth. "But let me tell you something wonderful, a mystery I'll probably never fully understand. We're not all going to die—but we are all going to be changed. You hear a blast to end all blasts from a trumpet, and in the time that you look up and blink your eyes—it's over. On signal from that trumpet from heaven, the dead will be up and out of their graves, beyond the reach of death, never to die again. At the same moment and in the same way, we'll all be changed." (1 Corinthians 15:51-52, MSG) If you are trusting Jesus as your Savior, you will be part of this group that leaves before the judgment. Think about it and trust Him before its too late.

Enemies

A family in my church was robbed last week. They placed their outgoing mail in their mailbox, which included several checks to pay some bills. A thief pilfered the mailbox and removed the checks. A few alterations, a false ID, a trip to a local bank and my friends were fleeced. With all the hi-tech methods we have to protect ourselves from thieves, who would have thought the lowly mailbox was at risk?

We think we are secure and some small chink in our armor makes us vulnerable. Locks were designed to keep the honest folks out. It's the small things that cause us the biggest problems. The unexpected. The "I-never-thought-about-that" events. Just when you feel secure, your security is stripped away. That's the way life is at times. True security is not found in locks and weapons. It's found in a dependence and faith in God.

Thieves may steal your stuff but you can stop them from stealing your joy. The family that had their mailbox violated asked me to pray for the people who did the crime. "They need the Lord," was their prayer. Now that's the attitude the bible speaks about. "Love your enemies." "Do good to those who despitefully use you." "If your enemy slaps you, turn the other cheek." How are you able to have this biblical approach and attitude to those who intend you harm? You come to the realization that you are vulnerable all day long. "Some trust in chariots and some trust in horses. But we trust in the name of the Lord our God." (Psalms 20:7, NIV) Where is your trust today? If you are depending on locks and weapons for protection, you will be disappointed and turn bitter when you are harmed. Put your trust in God. He is all you will ever need. By the way, don't tempt God. Lock your doors and bring your mail to the post office.

Evidence of Jesus

"Mary Did You Know?" is a song written by Mark Lowry several years ago, and is fast becoming a Christmas favorite, along with Silent Night and Little Town of Bethlehem. Mark's lyrics list a whole raft of questions to Mary in the song, such as: "Mary did you know your baby boy would one day walk on water?" "…would save our sons and daughters?" "… is heaven's perfect Lamb?"   But the one that stirs my heart is, "Mary did you know when you kissed your little baby, you have kissed the face of God?"

Mark's questions are rhetorical because Mary is the only one who knew for sure that her baby was the Son of God. The angel Gabriel told Mary that she would conceive a son. Mary retorted, "How can this be since I am a virgin?" So, when Mary delivered her baby, she was, and is, the only person on the planet who knew for sure, because she experienced the miracle virgin birth. Joseph, her husband, believed it was true. The shepherds believed it was true. The Wise Men from the East believed it was true. Everyone who has ever heard the story has had to exercise his or her faith to believe what only Mary knew.

About 33 years after the first Christmas celebration in Bethlehem, a similar situation arose about Jesus. After He had been crucified, buried and resurrected, one of the Apostles, Thomas, refused to believe Jesus was alive. "So the other disciples told him, 'We have seen the Lord!' But he said to them, 'Unless I see the nail marks in his hands and put my finger where the nails were, and put my hand into his side, I will not believe.'" (John 20:25, NIV) A week later Jesus showed up where Thomas was and instructed Him to put his fingers into His hands, and his hand into His side. Thomas exclaimed, after he followed Jesus' instructions, "My Lord and My God!" "Then Jesus told him, 'Because you have seen me, you have believed; blessed are those who have not seen and yet have believed.'" (John 20:29, NIV)

Jesus was thinking about us on that awesome day with Thomas. Thomas believed because he saw, but Jesus spoke of us when He said, "…blessed are those who have not seen and yet have believed." The key to

Christianity is to believe by faith that Jesus is the Christmas baby, but also the Resurrected Christ, who took your sins upon Himself, thereby paying the penalty for your sins, and proving He was God when He rose from the dead. Do you believe? Only those who believe will ever see and touch Him like Mary and Thomas. Have a blessed and holy and faith-filled Christmas.

Family Values

Mothers are the most indispensable people on the planet. What if Aldous Huxley's book "Brave New World," written in 1931 predicting life set in AD 2540, were true? Motherhood would be no more as all children would be born in a test tube. Without moms who would: Kiss your boo-boo? Tuck you in at night? Teach you how to walk? Sing? Kiss? Hug? Show you wonders in the clouds? Love you all the time? Teach you right from wrong? Be your biggest fan? Call you on your birthday? Fight for you against all odds? Cry for you? Yes, your life would be a lot different and much poorer without mom.

It seems from the beginning of time moms have been the targets of evil. Eve, the mother of all men, was tempted to sin before anyone else. Mothers have been pushed out of the safety of their nest to fend for themselves in the world. The prods are phrases like: "You can have it all," or "You're as good as any man," or "We need the extra money." I think you get the picture. Then moms really became the targets with the words, "Women have the right to choose." Then moms became complicit in murdering their children through abortion. You see, the plan of evil has been to destroy the greatest gift to society – motherhood. Who is going to protect mom?

Where are the men who stand as a shield to protect their mothers and the mothers of their children? Where are the men who say you can't use that language around the women in my life? Where are the men who are willing to give their lives to make sure motherhood is preserved and protected? Did you ever notice that when Jesus was dying on the cross, the last piece of business He addressed was to make sure John took care of His mother?

We need to resurrect the paradigm where mothers are honored, protected and respected once again. We need to hail motherhood as the greatest institution in the world, and whenever that institution is threatened, to be vocal and active to preserve it for the next generation. Let the cry of this generation be, "Mom, you can depend on us to watch over you." If your mom is around, do what you can to make this Mother's Day one she will remember. If she's gone, find someone else's mom to hug. I promise you, mothers will always love you.

Fasting

Have you ever fasted? No, not dieted but fasted. On a diet you suffer through various "programs" for a period of time, lose some weight, get tired of the regiment and back on goes the weight with little evidence of all you went through. A fast has to do with your spiritual weight not your body weight.

According to the bible, there are countless incidences where people fasted and had awesome results. Sometimes they fasted because of sickness. Others fasted to discover God's will. There were times when people were at war and needed victory over their enemies. Some were under attack by demon forces. Sadly, sometimes people had forgotten God and they were called on to declare a fast and get back to Him.

Should New Testament believers practice fasting? That's like asking should we give of our finances or should we pray. Fasting has a place in our Christian walk in that it helps focus our attention on spiritual things. We set aside a day or forty days or somewhere in-between to block out our busy lives. The benefit of fasting is not that it changes us into better Christians but that it helps us experience God and His blessings more intensely.

Churches don't teach much on this subject because people resist anything that keeps them from the pleasures of food. But it does us good to deny our appetites and spend time seeking God as we pray and fast. I recently called for the people in my congregation to join me in a 21 day fast. The results were fantastic! People had prayers answered as they were drawn close into God's presence. In fact it went so well that many have asked me when will we do it again. Imagine that! God's people fasting and praying. "Blessed are those who hunger and thirst for righteousness, for they will be filled." (Matthew 5:6, NIV)

Father's Day

There is a rumor spreading that Father's Day is going to be canceled this year due to a lack of deserving fathers. Oh, we have an abundance of biologically responsible creators of children but a severe shortage of true fathers. Can you name three things that would identify a man who is worthy to be honored on Father's Day? Note: you are not allowed to use matching DNA as a characteristic in your list. (Please make your list before reading any further.)

The first characteristic of a good father is that he loves and cares for his wife. "Husbands, love your wives, just as Christ loved the church and gave himself up for her." (Ephesians 5:25, NIV) A good dad has a model to follow in the way he is to love and care for his wife. That model is the way Christ cares for and loves His bride – The Church. Jesus did everything for the church. He gave His life for her. He gave instructions for her. He protected her. He showers her with His presence and undivided attention.

A second characteristic of a good father is that he takes responsibility for training and instructing his children in the ways of God. "Fathers, do not exasperate your children; instead, bring them up in the training and instruction of the Lord." (Ephesians 6:4, NIV) This is more than dropping the kids off at church or sending them to a Christian school. He knows the ways of God and takes the time to train and instruct his children – hands on.

A third characteristic of a good father is that he takes responsibility for his family. "Now I want you to realize that the head of every man is Christ, and the head of the woman is man, and the head of Christ is God." (1 Corinthians 11:3, NIV) He doesn't follow the trendy concept of family where everyone does as they see fit, but he accepts the God ordained mantel of leadership for his family. Not as a dictator who rules with an iron fist, but as a man of God who follows Christ and leads his family in Christ's pathway.

That's my top three. How does your list compare to mine? Dads, how about reversing the Father's Day tradition of receiving a gift and give one to your wife and children by reading this article to them and making sure every day is Family Day in your house. I was kidding about Father's Day being canceled.

Hallmark Cards and the tie industry would never allow that to happen.

Feelings

"I don't know how I'm going to preach today!" I exclaimed to my wife amid my tears. It all started when I was invited to preach at a very conservative church about 50 miles from where I lived. I had prepared my sermon like any of the others I had developed. But something different was happening to disrupt my spiritual awareness this Sunday morning. God seemed so close. I was keenly aware of His presence. I could not stop my eyes from filling with tears. In short, I was a mess.

My wife, in the interest of safety, took my car keys and put me in the passenger's seat. I wept and prayed the whole trip to the church. Upon arrival I was invited by the assistant pastor to sit on the platform with him during the music portion of the service. I declined his invitation and amid sniffles and salty tears and took a seat where no one could see my mysterious condition. The music started and ended and I was introduced to a packed house of a couple of hundred people who were attending the early service. I told God that I could preach or cry but I could not do both. His mercy ended the tears and I stepped behind the pulpit.

I preached the best sermon of my life! It was as if God was coaching every word and gesture I made. My sermon notes were unnecessary as waves of the Holy Spirit spilled over me. The 45 minute sermon seemed like a moment in time. I extended an invitation to the congregation to come forward to the front of the church to accept Jesus as their savior or any other prayer need they might have. I knew that we were about to see a great movement of God like few have ever experienced. The music was playing gently in the background. And... no one moved. Time stood still. The look on everyone's face told me to p-l-e-a-s-e let them go home. Disappointedly I did.

I went to the pastor's office and wept as the Holy Spirit swept over me waiting for the next service to begin. About one minute before the assistant pastor came for me my tears abruptly ended. The Spirit of God lifted from me. I was back into a normal reality. I sat through the worship music. I almost yawned I was so bored. I stepped up to the waiting pulpit and began to repeat my sermon from the first service. I forgot almost everything I had studied and prepared the previous weeks. I virtually read my notes. In less than 30 minutes I pronounced the final "Amen!" and could not wait to get to the restaurant to eat lunch. Then it happened.

A woman on the back row lifted and waved her hand and asked for permission to speak. She said she was prompted by God to read a verse from a song in the hymnal. I gave her permission. As she finished reading, a woman in the front row stood up and shouted, "That's for me!" as she rushed to the front of the church, fell on the carpeted floor and began to sob. Another person rose up and ran to the front of the church. Then the pews began to empty as person after person came forward for prayer and salvation. I just watched, amazed at what was happening. I was flat as a fritter and God was moving in a way I had never seen or experienced.

As I drove home somewhat bewildered from the morning's services I heard the voice of God speaking to me. He said, "The movement of His Spirit does not depend on how you feel. It depends on My sovereign power." I learned a powerful lesson that day: Everything depends on God and very little, if anything, depends on me. Today, you may feel depressed or sad. Perhaps you feel happy and elated. I can guarantee that how you "feel" does not energize or hinder the power of God to move it your life. It's all about Him!

First Commandment

Here's a thought for today. Under the Law, the greatest commandment according to Jesus, is to love God with your entire being and to love your neighbor as yourself. We often think we're doing okay with God by not murdering, or stealing or committing adultery. We delude ourselves into thinking we are keeping the Law and have gained favor with God. The truth is, we fail to love God as He deserves to be loved. In fact, it's impossible to love God as He deserves to be loved. We do not have that capacity in these fallen bodies we inhabit. We are a fallen race and cannot love God or anyone else as God wants us to love. We have all broken the first and greatest commandment.

This is why believers have been set free from the Law. We are by nature Lawbreakers. Jesus has ushered in a New Covenant that sets us free from the Law.

"Therefore, there is now no condemnation for those who are in Christ Jesus, because through Christ Jesus the law of the Spirit who gives life has set you free from the law of sin and death." (Romans 8:1–2, NIV) We are not condemned, because we are set free from the law of sin and death. Jesus set us free! We don't worry about loving God as described under the Law, because God demonstrated His love for us by sending His Son to die and set us free! We are to bask in the riches of His love for us. In the New Covenant, we believe that God loves us with all His heart, mind and spirit, and we receive that love. Only when we have Christ in us can we fulfill the admonition to love God, because Christ in us enables us to love God with the love of Jesus.

Think about this for a while and meditate on how much God loves you. Can you answer these questions? (1) How much does the Father love Jesus His Son? (2) If Father loves Jesus that much, how much does He love you, by giving His only Son to die for your sins? Now that's a lot of love being directed toward you!

Follow His Voice

Have you ever noticed how many times Jesus was involved with fish? He told Peter to cast his net on the other side of the boat after a night of fishing and catching nothing. Peter followed Jesus' instructions and caught a host of fish that almost broke his net. Another time, he took a few fish from a boy's lunch box and fed thousands of people. Jesus called many of His disciples from lives as fishermen and transformed them into fishers of men. Then after His resurrection, he fried up a meal of fresh fish on the shore of the Sea of Galilee for Peter and the despondent apostles who went on another fishing trip. Is there a common thread in all these fish encounters? I think so.

It's not about the fish, but what Jesus can do with fish and fishermen. He can herd fish into a net. He can cause fish in His hands to increase and feed thousands. He can call men to give up their livelihood and spend their lives catching men. He can prepare a banquet for men to eat. His voice is irresistible to nature and men alike. Fish rush from the safety of the water to the web of a net at His voice. Fish that are dead in a lunch box hear his voice and start reproducing in His hands. Men give up all to follow His call. Fish miraculously appear in his frying pan as He cries out to the disciples, "Do you have anything to eat?" It's His voice. He calls and heaven and earth respond.

When was the last time you heard His voice speaking to you? Was it in a time of danger when He whispered, "Fear not!" Was it when you were alone and he gently said, "I am with you." Had your world fallen apart and He encouraged you as He said, "I am the Prince of Peace." The voice of our Savior is ever calling and encouraging and directing those who will listen and respond. Why not swim upstream from the rest of the school of fish and respond to His voice. Put your life, your future, your past and your eternity into His hands. Here's a word from Jesus echoing through the ages to reach your hearing today. "Are you tired? Worn out? Burned out on religion? Come to me. Get away with me and you'll recover your life. I'll show you how to take a real rest. Walk with me and work with me—watch how I do it. Learn the unforced rhythms of grace. I won't lay anything heavy or ill-fitting on you. Keep company with me and you'll learn to live freely and lightly." (Matthew 11:28–30, MSG)

Forgiveness Bucket List

The Bucket List movie made all of us search our inventory of dream adventures that we have put in the wastebasket of time. One of the items on Jack Nicholson's Bucket List was to kiss the most beautiful girl in the world. The movie closed with him kissing his little granddaughter, who he had never seen, on the cheek as she tightly hugged his neck. That made everyone in the theatre cry.

The biggest failures of life are not doing something and failing to get some unrealistic result. It's failing to do what we wanted to do. The results are not nearly as important as the doing. I met a man several years ago who went on a trip across the world to climb Everest. He related every moment of his adventure, even to the crescendo of the story, when he said he did not make it to the peak. Some folks would say he failed. I didn't think so and neither did he. He was there! He experienced the cold! He was part of the team! He put a check mark on his Bucket List! Most of us don't have Everest on our Bucket List. Ours list may have: Visit grandpa before he dies.

Cruise somewhere. The vacation my wife wants. Go back to church. Read the entire bible. So maybe you won't jump out of a perfectly good plane, but there are things you can do that will bring vitality back into your life.

One attainable thing most people could do that would change their lives forever is to get forgiveness for what they've done wrong. I know all of us have hurt someone and wish we could say "I'm sorry, will you forgive me?" It may be your parents. Perhaps your children. A best friend. Yourself. God… I've learned that asking the question about forgiveness is more important than the answer you receive. You are not responsible for how others may respond to you. You are only responsible for what you do. Keep this thought in mind. Everyone may reject your apology. But God will never reject you when you ask Him for forgiveness. "On the other hand, if we admit our sins —make a clean breast of them—he won't let us down; he'll be true to himself. He'll forgive our sins and purge us of all wrongdoing." (1 John 1:9, MSG) In fact, I'd ask Him before I went to anyone else. That would be a magnificent check mark on your Bucket List.

Founding Father's Prayers

Last week I attended the Slidell Mayor's Community Prayer Breakfast at the Slidell Civic Auditorium. I had great expectations of this gathering to honor God. I found a good seat where I could watch the entire program unobstructed. The Principal of Slidell High School gave the opening greeting, a blessing over the food was prayed and we enjoyed a nice breakfast before the program began.

The written program listed the elected officials, most of whom were mayors of nearby cities, and I was excited to hear what they had to say. To everyone's pleasant surprise, as each speaker stepped up to the podium, they read a scripture verse and a prayer or statement from one of the Founding Fathers of the United States. We heard **President George Washington's** prayer from 1752, "…increase my faith, and direct me to the true object, Jesus Christ the Way, the Truth, and the Life." **President Thomas Jefferson** prayed in 1801, "In time of prosperity fill our hearts with thankfulness, and in the day of trouble, *let* not our trust in *You* fail; all of which we ask through Jesus Christ our Lord. Amen." **Elias Boudinot,** framer of the Bill of Rights, declared, "Therefore I move that some minister of the Gospel be requested to attend this Congress every morning . . . in order to open the meeting with prayer." **Abraham Lincoln** stated. "I know that the Lord is always on the side of the right. But it is my constant anxiety and prayer that I and this nation should be on the Lord's side." The audience displayed awe and appreciation as they heard the words of those who established this great nation. They were without doubt men of God, who unabashedly left public records of their dedication to God and their devotion to this fledgling nation.

The mayor of Slidell, the featured speaker, approached the podium and spoke, not as a politician or a preacher, but an ordinary man who had experienced the hand of God throughout his life. He said that he believed God had directed him to Slidell and the work that was entrusted to him as an elected official.
It was so refreshing to see those elected with authority over us as a community, from the Parish President to a

High School principal, publicly stating that we are still "One Nation Under God."

"Blessed is the nation whose God is the Lord, the people he chose for his inheritance." (Psalms 33:12, NIV)

Fragrances Have Meaning To Us

Have you ever smelled something that caused a rush of memories to flood your mind? It could be someone who walked by. The fragrance of a flower. Food cooking on a stove. A summer breeze filled with a soon coming rain. It actually happens all the time. The fragrance may remind us of something pleasant like a romantic dinner with your spouse. Or it may be a reminder of a painful situation from the past. In either case the fragrance sparks the memory and we deal with it – good or bad.

There is an interesting passage in the bible about a sweet bouquet that fills our senses that speaks about Christ. "God, who always leads us in triumphal procession in Christ andf through us spreads everywhere the fragrance of the knowledge of him. For we are to God the aroma of Christ among those who are being saved and those who are perishing." (2

Corinthians 2:14-15, NIV) Those of us who believe in Christ and have Him residing within us give off a fragrance of the Christ in us. Christ is referred to as the Lilly of the Valley and in another place as the Rose of Sharon. This passage reminds us of the beauty and aroma that radiates from Christ and vicariously radiates from Believers in Christ as well.

The aroma of Christ in you has two distinct effects. To other Believers it reminds them of the Christ in them. They identify with you and are reassured that they are filled with the eternal resurrected life of their Savior. Sadly, the unbelievers inhale the same fragrance and realize that they do not know Christ. The Believer's life and presence testifies to unbelievers that they do not have eternal life. "To the one we are the smell of death; to the other, the fragrance of life." (2 Corinthians 2:16, NIV)

The next time you sense that a stranger you just met is a Believer, it's the fragrance of Christ in them that you just inhaled. And the next time you meet someone and they treat you harshly, they may have rejected the waft of the fragrance of Christ that reminded them that they are among the perishing. Interesting fact of spiritual life isn't it?

Freedom

How did America become a free nation?

There is a War for Freedom being waged around the world. The cry to be free is a cry heard in every society known to man. Our founding fathers recognized this and heard the cry for freedom right here in the original colonies. The first settlers came here to be free but over a period of time that freedom was eroded and in 1776 men of great courage stood up and paid the price for freedom. Oddly enough they did not believe they had the power to bestow freedom on the people of the colonies. In the Declaration of Independence they declared that men were free because God set them free. But that freedom was maintained or secured by governments. "That to **secure these rights**, Governments are instituted among Men."

But where did they get such a notion of freedom? After all, most of the known world was not free. Most societies had dictatorships with a few rich powerful aristocrats who ruled over the masses using them to enhance their wealth and power. They got it, of all places, from the bible. Yes, that old out of date book, with ancient ideas that are so hard to understand (at least that's what lots of people think about it) held the message of true freedom. Jesus said it best when he declared, that He had come to set people free. But Jesus wasn't the only one to proclaim freedom. The Old and New Testaments are filled from cover to cover with heralds of freedom.

Virtually every pulpit from the first settlers on our shores to the crisis of 1776 proclaimed that men are free. Governments are created to maintain order and insure that freedom is not denied to anyone. They believed that America was to be the biblical "shining city on a hill" where men were free to worship God and live in harmony with each other. Look at what the Supreme Court of the United States said about government and freedom in 1892.

> *"Our laws and our institutions must necessarily be based upon and embody the teachings of the Redeemer of mankind. It is impossible that it*

should be otherwise; and in this sense and to this extent our civilization and our institutions are emphatically Christian." United States Supreme Court 1892, Church of the Holy Trinity Vs United States.

Well, much to the contrary of what a few uninformed leaders in Washington D.C. have said, America "is" a Christian Nation. I'll admit we don't act like a Christian nation much of the time. However, the bedrock foundation laid by Jesus declares it. And our forefathers declared it. And the Supreme Court declared it. Therefore, the evidence is sufficient to declare we are "…One nation, under God, indivisible, with liberty and justice for all." May God bless you and may God continue to bless the free and Christian United States of America.

Freedom of Speech

Where are the voices that speak out against immorality? Well, last week they were eating chicken at Chick-fil-A. This was a great opportunity for Christians to speak up doing what churches do very well. Eat! They didn't have to have a sit-in like in the days of Dr. Martin Luther King. They didn't have to get arrested for protesting at an abortion clinic. They didn't have to go to war as they did in 1776. No, they just had to eat some chicken. Did you go? I did, and it was a sight to behold. I went at 9:30 at night thinking I'd miss the crowd. I was wrong. The place was packed with Christians and those who believe in the First Amendment of the Constitution. And there were a few hungry chicken lovers who had no clue why so many people were in their favorite chicken place.

There were prayers over meals, Christian high-fives and "God bless you," proclamations to overworked Chick-fil-A employees across the nation. Why? Because Americans know that the fabric of society is a traditional home with a husband and a wife. Christians know the scriptures teach that marriage is between one man and one woman. And Americans believe in the Constitution and a person's right to free speech.

America rises or falls based on Christians' willingness to speak out. The churches were silent when they took the ten commandments out of public buildings. The pulpits were silent when prayer was removed from schools. You could hear a pin drop across America when the Supreme Court ruled it was okay to murder children in their mother's wombs. It seems the sleeping giant has awoke from its slumber and is ready to say once again that America is still "One Nation Under God."

There is a separation between church and state. But it's not what most Americans think that it is. The separation is a check-valve that only allows flow in one direction. The church can be involved in the affairs of the government but the government cannot interfere with the affairs of the church. "Congress shall make no law respecting an establishment of religion, or prohibiting the free exercise thereof; or abridging the freedom of speech, or of the press; or the right of the people peaceably to assemble, and to petition the Government for a redress of grievances." (First Amendment to the U.S. Constitution) The chicken eat-in last week was a legal expression of the right of Christians and Americans to peacefully express their views. I hope we see more of these kinds of demonstrations while we still can.

Friends

The best friends in life are the ones you can use. I know on the surface, when you first hear this, it sounds abrasive. Let me put it another way. "Its not what you know, but who you know." Yep, that sounds a bit rough too. Okay, maybe examples from real life are a better way to explain what I mean.

A good friend is one who is not annoyed when you ask them to do something that inconveniences them and costs them something of value. You may be borrowing something of significance to that person (i.e. their new Mercedes Benz). Perhaps you're asking your friend to help you with your project and they postpone their own project to assist you. Get the picture? A friend thinks you are more valuable than they are. The bible puts it this way: "Don't push your way to the front; don't sweet-talk your way to the top. Put yourself aside, and help others get ahead. Don't be obsessed with getting your own advantage.

Forget yourselves long enough to lend a helping hand. Think of yourselves the way Christ Jesus thought of himself. He had equal status with God but didn't think so much of himself that he had to cling to the advantages of that status no matter what." (Philippians 2:3-6, MSG)

Friends see the value in others and it gives them joy to help their friends. But maybe the greatest value of friends is they let you make mistakes and don't hold it against you. I told someone long ago who wanted to be my friend, and had professed his appreciation for me, that he would be my true friend when he loved me after seeing all my warts. He didn't understand what I meant at the time, but now that we have been friends for over 30 years, we love each other as only best friends can, knowing each other's faults/warts. The best friends never think they are being used. They take great pleasure in being with you. They are not afraid to let you see their shortcomings. They love you and let you love them.

I have lots of acquaintances but few friends that let me use them and feel free to use me. They are priceless. The passage of scripture above is a good mirror we can look into to see what kind of a friend we are. By the way, my best friend is Jesus. He loves me and loves to spend time with me. How cool is that?

Fruitfulness

I ate my breakfast cereal with sour milk today. I guess I need to tell you the whole story so you can appreciate how dumb it was to use sour milk. The cereal I eat for breakfast is my own special blend. I take three brands of cereal and mix them together with scientific precision. Then I add imported dried fruit that I discovered on board a ship about 20 years ago. I put this secret blend into a cereal bowl and top it with sliced banana or seasonal blueberries. Then I gently pour cold milk over my creation and enjoy my breakfast cereal. It is amazing! Why then would I pour sour milk over my creation?

Okay, this is a spiritual article so why am I writing about cereal? Because my foolish actions today are exactly what born again Christians do every day with their spiritual lives. God by His grace created you as a special delight for all creation to see. When you received Christ as your Savior everything about you changed. You are beautiful beyond description. You are dressed in royal robes of righteousness. You have designer sandals on your feet. You have a priceless family ring, the signet of God, on your hand. You have the Holy Spirit residing within you. All creation is speechless when they see what God has done in you. Then you pour sour behavior over God's creation.

There is an account in the book of Isaiah of God planting a vineyard, and all the work He did to make it fruitful. But it only produced sour grapes. God then asks the following question. "What more could I have done for my vineyard that I have not already done? When I expected sweet grapes, why did my vineyard give me bitter grapes?" (Isaiah 5:4, NLT) You are God's vineyard.

You live a spiritually fruitless life God never intended you to live. Why? Because you have never realized who you are in Christ. You don't see the value that God places on you. The day you realize how much God values you, and how great His plans are for you, then you will stop pouring sour milk over His creation. Start living the life He has prepared for you and you will see the glory of God in the sweet fruitfulness of your life.

Giving, Tithes and Taxes

The big question of the day is whether the United States will default on its spending obligations. If history is any indicator of the future, the United States government will find a way to spend more money. All the elected officials in Washington are chanting the mantra of Jerry Maguire, "Show me the money!" Problem is, there isn't any money. In the old days, the way to run a government was "tax-and-spend." Today its tax-borrow-spend and then raise the debt limit.

I like God's way of running the Kingdom better. "Those who don't work don't eat." "Bring your tithes into the storehouse." There was a couple who tried to cheat God, in the book of Acts, by lying about what they were giving to the Kingdom of God. St. Peter caught them in the lie and the next day they had a funeral for two. God's plan is simple. You work to earn a living. Everybody, yes everybody, gives the first ten percent (tithe) of what they earn to the Kingdom of God. Then low and behold, God gives back more than you give, so you can earn some more, and continue the cycle of giving and receiving. "Give, and it will be given to you. A good measure, pressed down, shaken together and running over, will be poured into your lap. For with the measure you use, it will be measured to you." (Luke 6:38, NIV) Now that's a plan I can vote for and live with.

Now some theologians will say we don't have to tithe since we are under Grace and not under Law. I wholeheartedly agree. There is no reason under the sun or in the bible that forces New Testament saints to give ten percent. You are free to give 20% or 30% or even more. The measure we need to use, is to give out of a cheerful heart. In other words give generously and feel good about what you're giving. By the way, there is no place in the bible where it says you are free not to give. I don't know if the United States government is going to default. You probably don't want that to happen. But you shouldn't default either. Give to the Kingdom. You won't be sorry.

Glory and Beauty

Several years ago, my wife and I went to Bellingrath Gardens in Mobile, Alabama. It was springtime and we went to see the azaleas in bloom. When we walked into the garden area we were overcome with an unexpected sight that I have never forgotten. The azaleas were in full bloom! Every branch on every bush had bouquets of flowers that filled our eyes with a symphony of color. We traveled from pathway to pathway and at every turn were greeted by more and more shades of bursting colors, that the most gifted artist every born would be unable to reproduce on canvas. It was a once in a lifetime experience that I have never encountered again.

I believe the disciples whom Jesus chose, felt the same way about Him as I felt that day in the garden. They said: "And the Word became flesh, and dwelt among us, and we saw His glory, glory as of the only begotten from the Father, full of grace and truth." (John 1:14, NAS) They saw what others have only dreamed of seeing. Moses, the great icon of the

Old Testament who climbed Sinai to be in God's presence, only saw His back for a moment. But the disciples saw His Glory. The Apostles Peter, James and John were awestruck when Jesus took them to a high mountain and allowed them to see what HE was really like. "And was transfigured before them: and his face did shine as the sun, and his raiment was white as the light." (Matthew 17:2, KJV) Can you imagine how many times they tried to recount that experience with others who were not there? Words are inadequate to describe reality.

Did you know that God was sharing the glory of His Son with every Believer in Jesus? Listen to this scripture: "All of us! Nothing between us and God, our faces shining with the brightness of his face. And so we are transfigured much like the Messiah, our lives gradually becoming brighter and more beautiful as God enters our lives and we become like him." (2 Corinthians 3:18, MSG) You are beautiful beyond description in Jesus. You reflect His glory every day. Just as an azalea bush conceals its glory until just the right time, your glory is being revealed day by day as He radiates through you. One day, at just the right time you will shed your mortal body and put on your eternal immortal body, and the total beauty of Christ, the Rose of Sharon, will be revived in you for all creation to see. So the next time you look in the mirror, look a little closer, and you might see the glory of God reflecting in your eyes.

God Cares For You

Are you glad the old year is drifting off into eternal history never to be repeated? Your answer depends on what happened to you last year. What if you had put a basket in your house and, whenever something good happened, you put a white pebble into it and, whenever something bad happened, you dropped in a black pebble. If I were to look in your basked what would I see? Lots of white, don't you think, with a few black stones mixed in?

The events that occur in our daily lives are mostly good (white stones) but for some reason we seem to remember the bad things (black stones) that happen. Why is that? We fall into the "Oh woe is me! I've had such a bad year," syndrome. Instead of being like the elephant that remembers everything, we act like the ostrich, which buries his head in the sand. Pull your head out of the sand and look around. Life is good!

The truth is that God showers down good into your life but you never realize it is God that is taking care of you or ever take the time to give Him thanks. There is an Old Testament book that deals with this subject titled "Hosea." Listen to what God had to say on the subject of His presence and goodness. *"I myself taught Israel (put your name here) how to walk, leading him along by the hand. But he doesn't know or even care that it was I who took care of him."* (Hosea 11:3, NLT) God was showering down good things, leading and teaching and taking care of His people, but they didn't know or even care that He was actively working in their lives. If fact they were giving honor to everyone and everything other than God for their lives.

Maybe you should get a basket and label it, "What God is doing in my life." Start putting those white and black pebbles into it for the New Year. I'll bet at the end of next year your basket will look like an Alaskan mountaintop covered with so much bright gleaming snow you won't be able to see any black stones anywhere. They may be there, but they will be buried under the goodness of God.

God Is Very Near You

I sometimes think life is like a Rubik's Cube. Just when you think you have all the colors lined up, a color swings into view that you didn't expect. Or, as my former business partner used to say about owning a business, "It's like putting on a blindfold and walking around on the interstate. No telling what might run over you." I suppose you've discovered by now that living on this planet can be dangerous.

However, God has a plan to bring calm into any and all situations. Isaiah, the Old Testament prophet, who by definition is a know-it-all, addressed the issue of God's intervention into the affairs of men. It was so poignant that Luke quoted it in the New Testament, "As it is written in the book of the words of Isaiah the prophet: "A voice of one calling in the wilderness,

'Prepare the way for the Lord, make straight paths for him. Every valley shall be filled in, every mountain and hill made low. The crooked roads shall become straight, the rough ways smooth. And all people will see God's salvation.' " (Luke 3:4-6, NIV) This statement was explaining how God could make order out of confusion. Deep valleys would be filled in. Crooked roads would be made straight. Rough going in life would be smoothed out. Then, everyone would know it was God who was at work making the impossibilities of life a holy reality.

You see, when you're in a deep dark valley, and every turn makes you feel lost and alone, and your teeth are jarring as you travel the washboard road, God promises to make a way for you through your wilderness. King David, of Goliath fame, said, "I've never seen the righteous forsaken." I could quote more scriptures than you would have time to read that proclaim that God is at work doing good things for you.

Slam on the brakes of life, take a deep breath, and listen for the voice of God saying, "Whether you turn to the right or to the left, your ears will hear a voice behind you, saying, 'This is the way; walk in it.'" (Isaiah 30:21, NIV) God is interested in you and is walking right beside you. Trust Him. By the way, I don't think even God can do a Rubik's Cube without getting a headache. Okay, maybe He can…

God Orders Your Steps

Remember the Zephyr in New Orleans? The first hump was slow with a steady click, click, click, as the gears pulled you ever closer to the top. Then there was a breathless moment of silence as the gears eased you over the edge and gravity took over from there. You screamed all the way down, as your heart rate went up, and you rode the famous Lake Pontchartrain amusement center roller coaster. Too bad it passed into history and that amusement park became a Hi-Tech office complex.

But all is not lost. New Years is a lot like the Zephyr. You get hurled from the holidays into the reality of a new year with all its twist and turns, racing and carrying you to events unknown. We never get to see very far ahead in life. Its all such a blur and we wonder if God cares about what's happening to us. Actually, God made a provision to help us see what is coming so we won't spend our lives screaming and out of breath. The provision is the word of God.

"Your word is a lamp to my feet and a light for my path." (Psalms 119:105, NIV) This scripture put into my language would read, "Your directions, according to what you have said, is a bright halogen light showing me the safety of the track before me, and it's so bright, I can see the curves ahead before I reach them." (Morris' Translation)

Do you get the picture? God doesn't allow you to get off track when you set your mind on following His instructions for your life as revealed in His Bible. There is security in knowing He is directing your life. He doesn't remove the curves so that you can see everything before it happens, but He lets you know that the safety of His tracks are around every curve of life. Knowing these facts takes the "scary out of life" to quote a current TV commercial.

God's Plan For You

I just got a new right arm. Seriously, I did get a new arm. My old one was worn out. Okay, just in case you don't know, I lost my right arm in a boating accident about 15 years ago. My right arm is now made up of computer chips, motors and all kinds of technical stuff designed to replace my right arm. The new arm is light years ahead of my old one. I can do tasks now that I have not done since I lost my flesh and blood arm. I can actually point with my index finger when I preach and want to get my point (excuse the pun) across. However, sad to say, modern technology can't come close to the original that God created.

Did you know that God created you? He did not just create mankind, but He created you. Abortion rights people refer to babies in the womb as "tissue," but God saw you as a person. Listen to this from the bible, "Oh yes, you shaped me first inside, then out; you formed me in my mother's womb. I thank you, High God—you're breathtaking! Body and soul, I am marvelously made! I worship in adoration—what a creation! You know me inside and out, you know every bone in my body; You know exactly how I was made, bit by bit, how I was sculpted from nothing into something. Like an open book, you watched me grow from conception to birth; all the stages of my life were spread out before you, The days of my life all prepared before I'd even lived one day." (Psalms 139:13-16, MSG) The wonder of all that God created when He made you is that He has plans for you life. "The days of my life were all prepared before I'd even lived one day."

God has been making plans for you since you first came into His mind. You're not just slime that crawled out of the primeval pond, but a person, created in the image of God, who is here on earth to do so much more than just breathe air. I believe, if you start seeing yourself as a person with a purpose, you will start appreciating the life God gave to you. Most people have low self-esteem because they don't see the value that God places on them. You are special! Ask God to let you see yourself as He sees you. It will change the entire pathway of your life. Oh, one last bit of advice. Don't get out of the boat when the motor's running.

God's Plan vs Yours

What should you do when your plans get uncontrollably changed? Get mad? Plan to get even? Get frustrated? Get over it? I suppose on any given occasion we have experienced any and all of these emotions. I don't like it when my plans change and I can't do anything to keep them from changing. Delayed flights when I need to get somewhere. A car that won't start. Sickness. Other antagonizing people. The list goes on and on.

There are several biblical solutions to these situations. You can thank God. Why? Because you won't know until you get to heaven what trouble you have avoided. Every once in a while someone will tell the story of how they just missed an accident because their car would not start. The bible says that God directs the steps of the righteous. He is not watching us to find a reason to punish us for our behavior. He is watching over us to protect us from evil.

I know that at times bad things happen and God gets the blame. But sometimes what we think is bad is actually good. Time has a way of letting us see the forest of life instead of just the trees. We look back and see that a great good came out of seeming tragedy. The best illustration of this is the death of Jesus. We look at the cross and wonder how God could stand by and let His Son suffer so much? Let's ask the thief on the cross next to Jesus what he thinks of the sufferings of Jesus. I know he would say if Jesus were not on the cross next to him he would be spending eternity in hell. Get the picture?

Try this. The next time "your" plans get changed, ask God what better plans He has for you. Start looking around and try to see what He sees that you don't. You may find that your delay created one of the best moments of your life. "And we know that in all things God works for the good of those who love him, who have been called according to his purpose." (Romans 8:28, NIV)

Good Friday

Black Friday is here. It seems strange to me how certain days get named something special. If a man from Mars were to land here and see all the Black Friday advertisements, he might think something bad was happening and get back in his trusty spaceship and head for home. How would you explain to him that it was good to be here on Black Friday. It is the greatest day of the year to shop for things. No matter that you don't need those things. Electronics, clothes, toys etc. can all be bought at supposed fantastic deals. The credit cards move from high balances to even higher balances. People finally go home with their cars stuffed with stuff and sit down in exhaustion after a day of spending money and say they were "saving" it. And at the end of Black Friday everyone is better off. Maybe not!

There is another oddly named Friday in our society. We call it Good Friday. Now that must be a really great day to be alive. What's so special about it? Well, as the story goes, the catalyst for naming it "good" Friday was that an innocent man who had never broken any laws was hauled before the judge and accused of every kind of crime. They took this innocent man and beat him to the point of death. And when they tired of their games, they nailed him to a cross. Then they jeered him to hurry up and die. After several hours the man finally died. What's so "good" about that kind of cruelty? They ought to call that Friday "black."

So why is there a Black Friday and a Good Friday? It's Black Friday because the retailers all move from the "red" (losses) to the "black" (profits). They call it Good Friday because the innocent man who died made it possible for "dead" people to become "alive" people. He became sin so that you could be made "good." It's called Good Friday not because what happened to Him was good. They named the day "good" because of the good that happens to you when you place your faith in Him. Think of it this way. He gave you the department store and everything in it for free. Now that's really a "Good" Black Friday.

 ## Gospel to Rome

Paul the apostle and I have something in common. He wanted to go to Rome and I want to go to Rome. Paul finally made the trip but he went in chains. I think the only way I will get there is the same manner. So with that in mind I thought it would be fun to cruise to Rome via Paul's writings – The Books of Romans.

Paul had an agenda in wanting to visit Rome and it wasn't to visit the Coliseum or other visual delights the Romans had constructed. He wanted to bring a gift to the people of Rome. He said, "I long to see you so that I may impart to you some spiritual gift to make you strong." (Romans 1:11, NIV) Normally, when people visit the Eternal City they want to bring some delight to remember the Roman adventure back home. Not Paul, he believed that he had something to offer to the citizens of Rome that would make them stronger.

Now when you think about the ancient Roman Empire do you ever think of them as weak or in need of some elixir to give them strength? Heavens no! They were the most powerful, influential and wealthy people on earth. But Paul knew the Romans had a chink in their armor. He started out his famous letter to Rome by pointing out their inherent problem. He described the proud Romans this way: "For although they knew God, they neither glorified him as God nor gave thanks to him, but their thinking became futile and their foolish hearts were darkened. Although they claimed to be wise, they became fools" (Romans 1:21-22, NIV)

Does Paul's indictment of Rome sound like an indictment to America? Look at the list: They knew God; They gave no glory to God; They gave no thanks to God; They had futile thinking; Their hearts were darkened; They claim to be wise; They became fools. Paul could have addressed his letter to the people of the United States.

What was the gift Paul wanted to give to Rome? He identified it when he said, "I am so eager to preach the gospel also to you who are in Rome." (Romans 1:15b, NIV) The only power than could transform the people of Rome was the gospel of Jesus Christ. What was true of Rome is also true of America. Why not join me in telling as many people as we can about Paul's Roman adventure and the Gospel of Jesus that can transform a nation. The Gospel is not the presentation of an idea, but the operation of the power of God to transform sinners into saints and nations into the Kingdom of God.

Government and Elections

When the national elections for President and Vice-President of the United States occur, there is often much debate about who will win. If I could answer that question prior to the post election announcement, I would be the smartest man on the planet. The men and women who understand the most about election polls are often scratching theirs heads until the announcement is made. Shortly after the announcement, they will be either busting their shirt buttons in pride because they were right, or they will be drooping their heads in shame because they were wrong. But I know someone who knows who will win the election before it's over, but He's not telling. God!

I have a night of worship and praise to God scheduled the day after the election each election year at my church. I schedule this not because I know who is going to win, but because no matter who wins, I intend to shout praises to God. Governments have a measure of power and authority, but they derive that power from God. I believe that God is interested in America because I believe He had a hand in its formation. Christopher Columbus believed God was sending him to the New World. The first settlers believed that God was sending them to establish the New World. The New World and the new government were established upon the Word of God and the will of God. Our nation has been known as a Judeo-Christian government since the ink was still wet on the founding documents.

You might either be shaking with joy or fear over the outcome of an election. But God and the Kingdom of God are not shaken one bit. It's more important that we have a nation under God than have a President Anybody. God is in control!

The scriptures say: "Some trust in chariots and some in horses, but we trust in the name of the LORD our God. They are brought to their knees and fall, but we rise up and stand firm. LORD, give victory to the king! Answer us when we call!" (Psalms 20:7-9, NIV) You see, chariots, horses, and kings are important, but the strength and victory of any nation depends on the Lord our God. Pray for our newly elected Presidents.

They will need divine wisdom to steer this mighty and awesome nation through the difficult times ahead.

Government and Taxes

The religious leaders of Jesus' day were always working for ways to trap Him. They wanted Him to say something they could use to discredit, imprison or put Him to death. Jesus being way smarter than His adversaries didn't fall for their tricks. He was like the cat playing with a mouse or in this case a rat. They did things like ask Him a loaded question and no matter which way He would answer, they had sprung a trap. He, on the other hand, would say things to entrap them like, "Okay, I'll ask you a question and if you answer correctly, I'll answer your question." Needless to say, they never had the right answer. Jesus would push the "beep" button sounding the wrong answer alarm. You can almost hear them muttering to themselves, shuffling away, their heads hung low wondering how He "got" them again.

One day they devised the master plan of entrapment. It must have been near April 15 when all tax returns had to be sent into the Roman IRS (Irreligious Rats

Association). They asked Jesus if it was lawful to pay taxes to the hated Roman government. Knowing Jesus was a "Holy" man and holy men hated the Romans, He would answer "No!" and they would have Him as an insurrectionist. If He said, "Yes!" He could be discredited as a Roman loving hypocrite. Jesus, smiling to Himself, asked for a Roman coin. Using His "ask them a question" technique, He asked whose inscription and image was on the coin. "Caesar," they chimed in unison, probably in the form of a question, knowing things were about to go bad. Jesus, flipped the coin back to them, and as it spiraled through the air into their hands, He said, "Render unto Caesar the things that belong to Caesar and to God the things that are God's. They just shuffled away again.

What does that story have to do with you? Lots! Believers, we live in two worlds. We owe our allegiance to government and we owe our allegiance to God. God establishes governments for the good of the people. We are to honor God ordained governments. "For the one in authority is God's servant for your good. But if you do wrong, be afraid, for rulers do not bear the sword for no reason. They are God's servants, agents of wrath to bring punishment on the wrongdoer." (Romans 13:4, NIV) Governments have authority for the "good" of the people they govern. Any official who enforces laws contrary to God and the good of His people, loses his/her right to govern. Jonathan Mayhew, the revolutionary preacher, patriot and commissioned officer, whose statue graces the United States Capital building, said in part, *"All commands running counter to the declared will of the supreme legislator of heaven and earth, are null and void: And therefore disobedience to them is a duty, not a crime."* (Jonathan Mayhew, 1740, Unlimited Submission and Non-resistance to the Higher Powers) Thank God, that our founding fathers established this great nation on Christian principles. So with all that said, when April 15 comes around this year, it'll be time to render unto Washington the things are Washington's....

Grace and Rest

"You load sixteen tons and what do you get? Another day older and deeper in debt. St. Peter don't you call me cause I can't go. I owe my soul to the company store," sang a popular voice from the past, Tennessee Ernie Ford. Kind of hopeless, don't you think? It sounds like all work with no reward, depression, heavy loads, and heaven a place you don't have time for. I don't think Mr. Ford knew how well he was describing contemporary America.

However, there is a better way to live. "Come to me, all you who are weary and burdened, and I will give you rest. Take my yoke upon you and learn from me, for I am gentle and humble in heart, and you will find rest for your souls. For my yoke is easy and my burden is light." (Matthew 11:28–30, NIV) The operative word in living a better life is, "come." Such a simple word that we use every day. To our children we say "Come here," when we want to give them something or keep them from danger. We invite friends to a meal when we say, "Come to my house for dinner." Jesus uses it to describe life on His side of life. "Come to me..." What an invitation from the Creator of the Universe and the Savior of the World. Where He is there is peace, rest, hope and a life filled with His perfect advice.

Can you imagine for just a moment what it would be like to be walking through life with Jesus? He sees danger before you do and warns you. He knows His perfect plans for your life and shares them freely. He teaches you the principles of the Kingdom of God so that you can avoid the pitfalls of the world. He calms the storms that come against you. He heals your sicknesses. He delivers you from evil. He will never leave you. He will never send you away. Does this all sound too good to be true? That's why we call life on Jesus' side of the street – Amazing Grace. The Bible closes with this invitation: "The Spirit and the bride say, 'Come!' And let the one who hears say, 'Come!' Let the one who is thirsty come; and let the one who wishes take the free gift of the water of life." (Revelation 22:17, NIV)   Why not drop that sixteen tons of weight and come to Him today? You will be amazed!

Groundhog Day and Forgiveness

Groundhog Day is here. The largest Groundhog Day celebration is held in Punxsutawney, Pennsylvania and folklore has it that if the local celebrity groundhog, Punxsutawney Phil, sees his shadow, there is more winter ahead. If not, we can break out the beach balls and get ready for summer. Hmmm… I think I'll stick to the weather channel and see what the experts have to say.

There was a movie made a few years ago named "Groundhog Day." The premise of the movie was that main character of the movie, played by Bill Murray, was stuck in a time warp. Each day when he woke up he was repeating the previous day, which happened to be Groundhog Day. It was frustrating to say the least. The only way for him to get out of the horrid time loop was to live a perfect day and do everything right. Sounds easy enough but, as the movie proved, it's a lot more difficult than you would think. Hollywood being what it is, they had mercy on Bill Murray's character and he finally got it right and went on with the rest of his life and thankfully ended the movie.

Did you know that God expects you to be perfect? Yep, that's the bad news from the bible. The only way to ever see God is to be perfect and sinless. I have a problem because I'm stuck on Groundhog Day like Bill Murray. I do my best to not fail God, but regrettably I fail every day. The great Apostle Paul said that he struggled with his behavior and was in a "Groundhog Day" spiral he could not escape either. If Paul was in trouble you know we're in trouble. Paul finally said that the only hope was what Jesus did for us. When we choose to believe in what Jesus did and receive Him into our lives as our Savior, God no longer sees us as sinners but as saints in Christ. When we are born again, we become perfect in His sight in Christ. You see, the perfect Son of God died on the Cross so that we could be forgiven and become the righteousness of God in Christ. You escape the spiral of sin when you confess your faith in Christ and invite Him to control every day of your life. "If you declare with your mouth, 'Jesus is Lord,' and believe in your heart that God raised him from the dead, you will be saved." (Romans 10:9, NIV)

Guarantees

"Nothing is guaranteed in this world!" is a saying we've all uttered at one time or another when our plans didn't work out. The biggest disappointment we've experienced is when someone you love fails again to follow through on an "I swear" promise. Yep, the only thing you can be sure of is the old death and taxes. No wonder we've turned into a society of skeptics.

I think King David, the hero of the Old Testament, must have felt the same way we do when he wrote, "I would have lost heart, unless I had believed that I would see the goodness of the LORD In the land of the living." (Psalms 27:13, NKJ) David found the only thing he could really trust was God. God never fails! Friends fail, things fail, health fails, and a host of other things we depend on fail, but God never fails.

One of my favorite scriptures says it best: "Yet this I call to mind and therefore I have hope: Because of the LORD's great love we are not consumed, for his compassions never fail. They are new every morning; great is your faithfulness." (Lamentations 3:21–23, NIV) Because God loves us, the undependable circumstances of life will not consume us. Because God's compassion will never fail, we can depend on Him to understand what we are going through in life. Because every day is a new day with God, and He is faithful to always be there for us, we can trust His faithfulness.

Quite a contrast between this world's guarantees and God's dependability, don't you agree? And God's guarantees go beyond this world into the new world. He promises that all our sins have been accounted for in Jesus' sacrifice on the cross, when He took all sins and their penalty upon Himself. He promises that whoever puts their trust and faith in Jesus would never die but inherit eternal life. Jesus said that one day He would return to planet earth and gather everyone, those who have died, and those who are still alive, to live with Him. We call it the Resurrection. I guess when you think about it, we can't depend on this world's guarantees, but we can stake our lives and all eternity on God's promises. All this makes me feel better about the disappointments I've experienced. How about you?

Have You Been Born Again?

Have you ever known anyone who came back from the dead? I don't mean a close call where someone stops breathing for a few minutes, but someone who was dead for days. I've read about a few cases, but to tell the truth I'm a bit of a skeptic. There is of course the story about Jesus' friend Lazarus in the bible. He was real sick and sent word for Jesus to come and pray for Him. By the time Jesus got there, Lazarus had been dead four days. Jesus called for Lazarus to come out of the grave, and low and behold the dead man stumbled into the light of day wrapped in the cocoon of still fresh grave clothes. That had to be the talk of the town for years to come. In fact, we're still talking about it 2,000 years later.

The Apostle Paul gave an account of masses of people coming back from the dead that is still occurring today. He was writing to a group of believers at Ephesus and said, "But because of his great love for us, God, who is rich in mercy, made us alive with

Christ even when we were dead in transgressions—it is by grace you have been saved." (Ephesians 2:4-5, NIV) We tend to look at life from a three dimensional perspective and declare people dead based on breathing and brain waves. Paul saw things from a better perspective and went on to say, "They are darkened in their understanding and separated from the life of God because of the ignorance that is in them due to the hardening of their hearts." (Ephesians 4:18, NIV) He believed that eternal life was found only in God and if God did not live in you, then you were devoid of true life.

What if Paul was right? Would it be worth the risk to die without the eternal life of God residing within you? What if the odds were that Paul was only 50 percent right? 40 percent? 10 percent? Let me put it this way. What if there was only a ten percent chance the next time you boarded a plane it would fall out of the sky, would you fly anyway? Why risk eternity on the chance that Paul is right? Invite Jesus into your life and see if you find signs of eternal life dwelling in you that you never thought possible. The next voice you hear might be Jesus calling you to come out of your living grave to spend eternity with Him.

Have You Seen Any Angels Lately?

I had an encounter with an angel recently. The one I met did not have wings, he was not nine feet tall, and he was not carrying a sharp pointed sword. The angel said his name was Dave. He was about 5' 6", probably in his fifties, wore a blue Walmart looking smock with several mandatory pins including a cross and a flag, and had a name tag with his picture on it. The best part of his cover was a U.S.M.C. tattoo on his forearm. I met Dave at the local hospital surgical waiting room. He was posing as an information volunteer assisting those whose loved ones were in surgery.

Every time the door to the waiting room would open, the angel, AKA Dave, greeted each person who entered with words like: "Welcome to Walmart!" Or "You'll come on in now!" using a slight Cajun accent.

Some who entered knew Dave was an angel because they had met him before. They would break out in a gigantic grin and say, "Oh, No! You're still here?" as if they though he might have gone back to heaven. Others who entered were very sad faced with furrowed brows, glancing into the room as if they were entering a place of great sorrow. Dave would escort them to a seat and say with a sheepish grin, "Your patient number is on the TV Surgery Status Monitor on the wall. Green means the Doctor has not started the surgery. The little zipper icon next to your number opens when surgery starts and your number will turn red. When the zipper closes, the surgery is over, and the number turns blue." Dave continued to inform and entertain about 20 people for over three hours non-stop. He would crack jokes. Do a funky camel walk dance. And perform hosts of other professional stand-up comedy routines that keep everyone in stitches. (Excuse the pun.)

And in the midst of all his humor, Dave would answer the phone, go to the surgery unit across the hall, and come back with reports on each person's loved one. Dave always got very serious when doctors would open the door and call for Mr. or Mrs. So-and-So, to come out into the hallway for the long-awaited news. He would crack the door a bit, and watch carefully, to make sure everyone was okay as they spoke with the doctors.

I am not sure the hospital knows Dave is an angel. They probably think he is just a volunteer giving out information. But I know he's an angel on assignment. In fact, the bible speaks about just such angel encounters as I had today. "Do not forget to show hospitality to strangers, for by so doing some people have shown hospitality to angels without knowing it." (Hebrews 13:2, NIV) Take a careful look around today. You may see an angel as you go about your daily life. They won't look like angels, but they will act like someone God sent into your life just when you needed it.

Heaven
Destination

Do you know where you're going and how to get there when you go on a trip? I used to travel by sense of direction while my wife was begging me to "Pleeeeease stop and ask someone." I just hate to ask for directions. But that was long ago. Now I have a GPS and Google to get me there. I drive to the sounds of "Recalculating. Make a U-turn at the next intersection," as Chatty, (my name for the GPS) does her best to get me to my intended destination. However, as those of you who have a GPS in your car know, the directions don't always get you there the fastest or shortest way. Even Google gurgles at times, and misses the mark.

Now, where you are going when you leave for a trip is important, but not nearly as important as making sure your "final" destination is established. It amazes me that so many people are hoping they get to heaven and trust their respective religious beliefs to get them "somewhere" at the end of life. They rely on what they "think" is right much like Chatty relies on the electronic map in her memory to get me to wherever I want to go. Now, its okay if Chatty misses the target since I can always swallow my pride and ask someone for directions, but what about the "Final Destination?"

You need to know where you are going at the end of life. St John wrote in his letter, "I write these things to you who believe in the name of the Son of God so that you may know that you have eternal life. (1 John 5:13, NIV) John made it clear that "you who believe…may know that you have eternal life." You can know your final destination and not be guessing and hoping and thinking you might make it to heaven. The last trip you make will be the most important. A man in the book of Acts asked St. Paul for direction to his final destination. He asked, "What must I do to be saved?" St. Paul answered, "Believe on the Lord Jesus Christ and you will be saved." (Acts 16:30-31, NKJ) Do you believe? If not, ask Jesus for direction to heaven right now, and commit to follow His direction all the days of your life. Have a great trip!

Heaven's Crown

The Amazing Race for the gold begins. People from all over the world will stream into the selected city to watch and cheer as the best qualified athletes on the planet go head to head, in the world's most prestigious athletic competition – The Olympics!

I think St Paul was a sports enthusiast. The Olympics began in Olympia Greece about 776 B.C. Paul doesn't say if he ever went to the "real" Olympic games but I suspect he knew about them and loved to muse about the great athletes of his day. When he wrote the letters that became our bible he often spoke of races, boxing, training and similar metaphors, to drive home some spiritual point. Today, he might have said going to heaven was like winning the Super Bowl.

Paul uses the Olympic trophy to compare what has the greatest value in the competition of life. "Everyone who competes in the games exercises self-control in all things. They then *do it* to receive a perishable wreath, but we an imperishable." (1 Corinthians 9:25, NAS; emphasis mine) The athletes of his day did not win a gold medal but a plaited wreath that quickly died and crumpled away. Jesus said this same thing another way: "For what will it profit a man if he gains the whole world and forfeits his soul? Or what will a man give in exchange for his soul?" (Matthew 16:26, NAS)

We work so hard to gain earthly trophies and a reputation that no one will remember next year. But the most important crown that we must obtain will never fade or lose its value. That crown is the crown of life awarded to everyone who believes on the Lord Jesus as his or her Savior. At the end of Paul's life he said he had run his race and finished his course. He knew that he had won the ultimate trophy in life. He had won entrance into the heavenly hall of fame. How about you? Your entrance into heaven has been won already. Jesus crossed the finish line of victory for you and invites you to join Him on the winner's podium.

Helpless

"Help, I've fallen and I can't get up!" was the tag line in a commercial several year ago. We all sort of picked up on it and repeated it ad infinitum, until finally, we went on to other popular clichés. But that overworked expression was filled with more truth than we are willing to admit. Many people around the world are on their knees either because they fell or some bully or event in life pushed them down. Where are the heroes on white horses who are riding in to rescue them? Much to our shame we have put earplugs into our ears, masks over our eyes and turned in the other direction to avoid the cries for help.

Jesus addressed this issue when he told the story about the man who had been beaten, robbed and left to die. Everyone walked by. The religious leader. The businessman. The people in a hurry. The ones who did not want to look at the unsightly sight. Then a man, who most people would have shunned, a half-breed who was rejected by society because of his ethnic background, stopped and gave assistance to the fallen man. When Jesus told this story, everyone hung their heads in shame and eased away hoping to do escape the piercing gaze of Jesus.

Countless thousands of people are suffering today. Human trafficking, child abuse, suicide, etc. are rampant in the world and in our towns across America. Who is stopping to give them assistance? Some would say, "Let God do it!" God would reply, "Who will go for me?" The truth is that those who are Believers in Jesus are His eyes, hands, ears and heart. He wants to help the helpless and He wants to do it through you. "When He saw the crowds, He had compassion on them, because they were harassed and helpless, like sheep without a shepherd." (Matthew 9:36, NIV) The next time you see someone in need why not go to them and offer a helping hand? Maybe no one will notice what you've done except Jesus. He will never forget that you helped the helpless.

Holiday Season

"Gentlemen, start your engines!" is the announcement made at the Le Mans racetrack. We could almost say the same thing as we start the holiday season. Thanksgiving starts it off with food and thanks to God and New Years ends it with thanks to God that the holidays are finally over. Why is celebrating Thanksgiving, Christmas and New Years so tiring? Maybe its because we overeat, over-drink, overspend and overdo everything? Hmmm….

Remember the wonderful Christmas songs like "Silent Night" and "Away in a Manger?" We replaced them with "Jingle Bells" and "Rudolph the Red Nose Reindeer." What about that calming message of the angels as they announced "Peace on earth." We've changed that to "piece of pumpkin pie." We not only start our engines, we race away to crash and burn on the first turn.

I have a new way to start the Christmas season. "Gentlemen, start your memories." Yes your memories. Remember that Thanksgiving is about thanking God for the wonderful provisions He has given you. Stop looking for something else to buy! Remember that Christmas is about God doing something to save the world from sin and trouble. Stop looking to Santa Clause to fill your stockings with more stuff you don't need anyway. If you truly needed it you would have bought it long ago. Remember that New Years is a time to refresh your focus on a new start. It's a time of forgetting your mistakes and making plans to do better next year. How about living the lyrics of the New Years Eve song "Auld Lang Syne" that translated from the old Scottish dialect means "Old Long Ago." The lyrics are in part: "We drink a cup of kindness, for old long ago." It's a time to remember friends and loved ones who are in our lives every day and make each year a better one.

This season, stop your engine and take a break. Enjoy yourself. Remember God. Remember those you love and who love you. Remember to enjoy the days of celebration and on January 2 of next year, you can whisper a quiet prayer of thanks, for all the good, peaceful, memorable times you experienced. You won't be sorry. How about this? "Ladies and gentlemen, stop…."

Holidays Are Coming

Did I see a Christmas tree lot opening on one of the main boulevards in town today? It must have been a dream. It could not possibly be Christmas. I'm still somewhere back on July 4th. I've seen movies where someone falls asleep and wakes up days or years later with no realization that time had slipped by. Maybe that's what happened last night when I went to bed.

Oh well, I can do this. Come on Thanksgiving and turkey! I'm ready for you Santa! New Years, I got a list of resolutions to make! Whew, maybe I'm not as ready as I thought. Just writing down those holiday names makes me weary.

The rushing of events is as old as the bible. When Jesus was making plans to depart planet earth He told His disciples that He would be coming back. They clamored with worried voices and asked Jesus when would that be. He said they didn't need to be concerned about the date of His return, but to be ready whenever He came. I think that's the way we need to lead our lives. We trust that God is in control and events will occur according to His timetable and not ours. We just need to wait upon the Lord and not be so busy building a time machine to rush things along.

The holidays will come and go in their good time. There's not a thing we can do to slow them down. Let's just take it one day at a time as much as possible, and close our eyes when we see Christmas trees in November. Oh, did I mention November is half over already? Yikes!

Holy Week

Next week Christian churches around the world will enter into what is termed as Holy Week. I love it! The non-Christian world is so devoid of the meaning of Holy Week, they can't muster an effective counter activity to it. The closest they have come is a bunny that lays colored eggs and an ample supply of candy for kids and adults. Bring it on! The more chocolate the better! And I love hard boiled eggs which the kids won't eat.

Days like Palm Sunday, Holy Thursday, Good Friday and Resurrection Sunday/Easter are anathema to the world. They certainly don't want to start the week with shouts of praise on Palm Sunday waving branches, which they can't eat. Holy Thursday? Sinners and holiness certainly don't mix. Good Friday? Mourning the cruel death of an innocent man is off the radar of the world. Unbelievers want no part of that day. That brings us to Resurrection Sunday. Celebrating a dead man coming back to life. No way!

So there you have it. Only believers and children are interested in Holy Week. Jesus said to bring the children to Him, so that's a great event for children. True believers mourn the death of Jesus, but celebrate the fact His death removed all their sins. And every believer is overjoyed that Jesus rose triumphant from the grave. The cross is empty, the tomb is empty and believers are filled with the Spirit of Christ. That's shouting ground for Christians.

Easter Sunday is a day when the churches will be filled. Find a good church to attend this year and join the celebration. Who knows? You might like it and start being a regular attender all year long.

How the Blind Can See

There are days when your life runs on autopilot and everything is the same old same old. You find yourself at work or in a store and can't remember how you got there. You glance at the clock and its time for the evening news. The day rushed by as if you were in some sort of time machine. None of the day's events were important enough to catch your attention. Then there are days when you are so sensitive to what's happening you have sensory overload. You lost your job. You fell in love. You won the lottery. The doctor said, "It's not cancer."

There is a man in the bible who was born blind and started his day on autopilot. Without any foreknowledge, he had a chance encounter with Jesus, who rubbed mud in his empty eye sockets, and the day took off like the Space Shuttle on a clear day. He could see! The entire town rocketed into orbit. Something that had never happened before became reality. A blind man could see. The formerly blind man was question by the authorities. He was grilled, maligned, accused of impersonating himself, told he was a demon worshiper and that the man who healed him was a sinner. Finally, in desperation he declared, "I don't know whether he is a sinner. But I know this: I was blind, and now I can see!"(John 9:25, NLT)

Toward the end of the day, Jesus found the elated and bewildered man, and asked him if he believed in the Messiah, with all the promises associated with Him. The man asked Jesus to show him this Messiah so he could believe. Jesus said "You are looking at Him." Wow! What a way to end the day. He began blind, was given his sight, and finished the day looking at The Messiah.

Jesus told His accusers that day, "For judgment I have come into this world, so that the blind will see and those who see will become blind." (John 9:39, NIV) Are you blind? The only way to see the world as Jesus and that blind man saw it, is to ask God to open your eyes to the reality of Christ. The blind man saw Jesus and believed He was The Messiah sent to open his eyes that he might see his Savior. The man was healed twice that day. First, his physical eyes were healed. Then, his spiritual eyes were opened. Why not follow that unnamed man's example and ask God to open your eyes to the reality of Jesus, who died for your sins, and invite Him into your life. Like the blind man you will see what you never saw before. By the way, if you need a physical healing you can ask for that too.

Hurricane Katrina

On August 28th 2005, my wife and I went to Picayune, Mississippi to avoid the category 5 hurricane named Katrina. Who knew the eye of the storm would pass over my good friend's house in which we were hunkered down? Two brave men, Art and myself, began to wilt as the velocity of the winds increased. Art, after several hours of severe battering causing thirteen trees to crash into his house, and his motor home to suffer damages, announced this unforgettable truth: "You are watching the birth of a wimp!" Yes, the wimp factor can rise higher than the storm surge during a hurricane. There are thousands of wimps now living along the Gulf Coast of the United States.

The truth is we don't like things we can't control and no one on the planet can control hurricanes. The weathermen give predictions as to how the storm will move, how powerful it is and how much damage it will do. But they can't steer it, lessen it, or make it go away. Jesus gave us a vivid description of what would happen at the end of the world. He described it in vivid detail so we could do something about it. We can't change it any more than we can redirect a hurricane. But we can get away from the effects of a storm and we can get away from the effects of the end times.

There is a shelter so strong that no storm, war, political upheaval, famine, persecutor, false prophet, fiery hail or murderous demons can penetrate. Jesus said, "For then there will be great distress, unequaled from the beginning of the world until now – and never to be equaled again. If those days had not been cut short, no one would survive, but for the sake of the elect those days will be shortened." (Matthew 24:21-22, NIV) Who are the elect who will be spared such devastation? They are everyone who puts their faith and trust in the finished work of Jesus. Jesus provides sanctuary from the end time tribulation for everyone who believes that He is the Christ, the Son of the living God. He is the shelter that cannot fail. Place your trust in Jesus before the storm arrives and it will be too late to run. Some say there will be no end of time. Some also say the hurricane won't hurt us. Get the point?

Hyper-Grace

I was introduced to a new word last week. It's a Greek word that was used by St. Paul in his letter to the Romans. He was in the middle of explaining how much more abundant and powerful Grace was as compared to the power of sin. He said that sin had come to mankind through Adam and was so powerful that it reigned and established control over fallen man. However, Grace came through Jesus and was much greater than the power of sin. The word I learned is used in Romans 5:20 - *"huperperisseúō."* I hope that Greek word didn't freak you out. It is a combination of two words, "huper" and "perisseuo" which translate in English as "hyper" and "abundantly." The translators of the New International Version of the bible used the phrase "grace increased all the more" to give us a verbal food fest of the abundance of Grace that God showers down upon the world. "The law was brought in so that the trespass might increase. But where sin increased, **grace increased all the more**, (Greek: *huperperisseúō*) so that, just as sin reigned in death, so also grace might reign through righteousness to bring eternal life through Jesus Christ our Lord." (Romans 5:20-21, NIV; emphasis mine)

Teachers and preachers who believe that Jesus is everything necessary for life and salvation many times refer to themselves as "Grace" teachers. Those who have difficulty agreeing with the Grace theology coined a new derogatory phrase to discredit them by referring to Grace teachers as "Hyper-Grace" extremists. I am by all measures a teacher of the Grace of God. So you can imagine my joy when I found that Paul first used the word "hyper" to explain the measure of Grace. The Grace of God is so abundant and so powerful Paul said it was Hyper-Grace. If you were to have a conversation with Paul and asked him if he believed in Hyper-Grace he might respond, "Is there any other kind?"

Why, you might ask, am I bringing *"huperperisseúō"* to your attention? I'm broaching the subject because the Grace of God is so much more than we think it is. When we use definitions of Grace and call it "unmerited favor" or "something you get that you don't deserve" it's comparable to calling the Hope Diamond a rock or gold dust as just dirt. The Grace of God is so powerful that it can cleanse away any sin, restore any sinner to God and build new life from any wreckage. Hyper-Grace alone can say from the cross, "Father, forgive them" as they executed Jesus. Hyper-Grace alone can say to an adulteress, "Neither do I condemn you." Hyper-Grace alone can say to any prodigal son or daughter, "This son of mine was dead, and is alive again. He was lost and is found." No matter where you've been, no matter what you've done, and no matter what you've said, Hyper Grace has the over abundant power to impart the Righteousness of God to you through Jesus alone.

Imaginations

"I can only imagine!" is a familiar phrase that we use all the time. We say this when we have difficulty "seeing" what actual reality will be like. My wife and I took on the unimaginable task of building a new house several years ago. This was our first (and last) attempt at such a monumental endeavor. Nothing turned out as we imagined it would. The cost was unimaginable. The plans were only a flat two-dimensional idea of what reality would be. In short, what we imagined was not reality.

Imagination is like an empty room in the recesses of our minds, and we fill that room with shapes and events as we suppose they will be. Some of the items in our cyberspace minds are good and some are bad. The good things are something we're going to build. What heaven will be like. A vacation we want to take. A job we'd like to have. The bad things are events that don't include God. An illicit love affair at the office. Vengeance against someone who hurt us. A plan to take advantage of someone. I think you get the picture.

Our imaginations can help us or hurt us. They help us by making us feel good about something in the future. Thus, the saying: "Getting there is half the fun!" It is bad for us when imaginations turn into worry about tomorrow. Scarlet O'Hara dealt with her imaginations of bad things by coining the phrase: "I'll worry about that tomorrow. After all tomorrow is another day." The bible offers us some assistance when our imaginations begin to control our lives in a negative way. "For the weapons of our warfare are not carnal, but mighty through God to the pulling down of strong holds; Casting down imaginations, and every high thing that exalts itself against the knowledge of God, and bringing into captivity every thought to the obedience of Christ." (2 Corinthians 10:4-5, KJV)

The weapons we can use that are able to bring our imaginations under the divine control of God are munitions that are standard issue to every believer. The bible has many instructions in dealing with the runaway imaginations of our minds. For example, it tells us what we should be thinking/imagining. "Summing it all up, friends, I'd say you'll do best by filling your minds and meditating on things true, noble, reputable, authentic, compelling, gracious—the best, not the worst; the beautiful, not the ugly; things to praise, not things to curse. (Philippians 4:8, MSG) So, I imagine, the best thing you can spend time imagining is what God has to say about your life. Clear out your minds and put in new thoughts about God and His plans for you.

Important Things

What's really important in your life? I mean what makes you wake up and want to get going. Is it your job? Is it your hobby? Is it your children? Grandchildren? Is it your spouse? Several years ago the movie "The Bucket List" was released. It was about the list of things you always wanted to do but never took the time to accomplish. What if you made a bucket list and completed every item on it, what then would be important in your life?

Life is more than what you do. What makes life important is who you are. Not your vocation or hobby but who you are. I had a job. I had a family. I had a bunch of stuff. But I had no sense of who I was or where I was going. I remember one night on August 7th 1972 when I couldn't sleep and I got up to check on my five year old daughter. She was sound asleep with not a care in the world. I knelt down next to her bed and began to cry. Something was wrong inside of me and I didn't understand what it was. The next day, August 8th, I discovered what was wrong.

"If you were to die, would you go to heaven or hell?" a stranger asked me that hot August day. I came face to face with myself and realized that the most important question in the Universe had just been posed to me. "If there is a heaven and a hell, then I would go to hell," was my response. The stranger, Jim, explained in about 20 minutes that if I would turn my life over to Jesus Christ, He would forgive all my sins and impart to me eternal life. He said I would be Born Again. I turned my life over to Christ that day and I have never been the same.

If you were to ask me today what was important in my life, I would not even have to think about it. It is Jesus Christ. You see, it's not that I'm important, it's that God believes I'm important. I'm so important to Him that Jesus gave His life so that I could have eternal life. Jesus said, "I am come that they [you] might have life, and that they [you] might have it more abundantly." (John 10:10, KJV) I believe that nothing will ever be really important to you until you discover how important you are to God. Why don't you invite Him into your life? You won't be disappointed. He might even help you make out a new bucket list.

Independence Day and Black Robe Regiment

The United States of America celebrates Independence Day with the boom of fireworks, the strains of patriotic music and big bites of barbecued hamburgers. The first Independence Day was celebrated with the cracks of rifle fire, the cries of the wounded and the cadence steps of British troops. The Founding Fathers, and those who took up arms for freedom, paid a heavy price to insure our God given liberty, as declared in the Declaration of Independence. But actually the first sounds of liberty were not from muskets but from the voices of the Black Robe Regiment.

The pulpits of the colonies were the tips of the sword that blazed the trail of freedom. Brave men stood before their congregations and proclaimed the injustices and anti-God decrees of King George III. The fire from the black robed preachers was so direct and lethal that King George III, in a back handed reference, named them the Black Robe Regiment. This became a rallying label and the battle cry. "No King But King Jesus," read the colonial newspapers and the Black Robe Regiment was created in history, and named as the leaders of the march to freedom.

Today, many Americans cry foul when the oracles of God speak out about anti-God government behavior as they raise the flag of The Separation Of Church and State. They do so in error. Nowhere in the Declaration of Independence or U.S. Constitution is it recorded that pulpits cannot interfere with the government. They only state that government cannot interfere with religion. (Article 1, Bill of Rights)

John the Baptizer set the pattern for the Regiment when he preached the Gospel and spoke against King Herod. He paid for these actions with his life. (Luke 3:18-20) The pulpits of the 1700s joined John and as they called King George III to task. (Declaration of Independence) Where is the Black Robe Regiment today? Wouldn't John and the Black Robe Regiment reprimand the pulpits of today that have been silent as prayer and the scriptures were ripped from our children in public schools? What would they say about the loud hush of the preachers as abortion was instituted by the black robe clad Supreme Court? Would they not be standing tall and bellowing with passion against a government that approves the destruction of the sanctity of marriage only between a man and a woman and replaces it with the biblically described forbidden fruit of homosexuality?

Charles Galloway, a Methodist bishop and church historian, expressed in 1898 of the Black Robe Regiment of 1776, "Mighty men they were, of iron nerve and strong hand and unblanched cheek and heart of flame. God needed not reeds shaken by the wind, not men clothed in soft raiment (Matthew 11:7-8, KJV), but heroes of hardihood and lofty courage. ... And such were the sons of the mighty who responded to the Divine call." (Charisma News, June 28, 2013)

Why not ask your pastor to put on his Black Robe and join the men of 1776 to speak out the Gospel of Jesus and the truth about our nation today. I have.

Integrity

How's your integrity? I'm referring to the old saying: Your word is your bond. A handshake means everything. You can be counted on to do what's right all the time. No one can justly accuse you of doing wrong. Would you score yourself at 90% on the integrity scale? 80%? Less? How would others score you?

The reason I am broaching this subject is because this quality seems to be slipping away from our society. The small print on the warranty card always seems to get you when the product you purchased doesn't work as advertised. The air miles you accumulated are only valid if you fly on the outside of the plane. Your boss can't remember that he promised you a raise. The politician you voted for is in jail.

When is it okay for you to renege on your word? When circumstances change, can you change what you promised? It happens all the time. I'm sure you have been the victim of lack of integrity.

It interests me that Jesus is called The Word. He said about Himself that He was The Truth. That means you can trust Him every day for all eternity to keep His Word. If He said it that settles it! Integrity would be a worthy quality to work on. Make sure if you say something you will do it. Make sure when someone depends on you to do right - you do it. Make sure that people are never disappointed in you. Now, I know that some people can never be satisfied. That's because they are severely lacking in integrity. Paul the Apostle addressed such issues. He said, "Never pay back evil for evil to anyone. Respect what is right in the sight of all men. If possible, so far as it depends on you, be at peace with all men." (Romans 12:17-18, NAS)

Here's the integrity test. When you lay your head on the pillow at night and you reflect on the day, before drifting off to sleep, can you say, "As far as I know no one is sleepless and worried because of the way I treated them today." If you can do that, you will have a nice night's sleep. If not, resolve that tomorrow you will try to make things right for that person.

Jesus is Alive

How do we know Jesus is alive? That is the most important question in all of human history. Yes, every Christian's faith depends on the fact that Jesus is alive. Otherwise Christianity is a hoax and we are in big trouble.

Can we know with any assurance that Jesus is alive? I say yes! Let's look at a few facts surrounding the resurrection and see if the resurrection is provable. First, the Roman soldiers who were sent to guard the tomb of Jesus would not have allowed the body to be taken away. Why? Because they would have been executed for dereliction of duty. Besides, do you think a band of believers led by Peter, with one sword, could overpower a Roman army contingent? Second, the Jewish leaders made up a lie that the body was stolen. Why would they make up that story if the tomb were not empty? The tomb was empty, but the question arises, where was Jesus' body? I think it is logical to assume if the disciples had the body that sooner or later it would have shown up. They would have wanted it to be revealed and possibly used as an icon of the Christian faith. If the Romans or Jews had the body they would have exposed the hoax of the Resurrection.

The undeniable facts are: Jesus died on the cross. Jesus was buried in the tomb. Jesus' body was missing. Jesus' body has never been produced. The only believable story is what the bible states – He had risen from the dead. There were eyewitness who died proclaiming Jesus was alive! "And that he appeared to Peter, and then to the Twelve. After that, he appeared to more than five hundred of the brothers at the same time, most of whom are still living, though some have fallen asleep. Then he appeared to James, then to all the apostles, and last of all he appeared to me also," (1 Corinthians 15:5-9, NIV) You can't get that many people to lie and be willing to die if they had not seen Jesus after the cross.

Lastly, and most importantly, I know Jesus is alive because of what He has done in my life. I was changed by His presence when I asked him to forgive my sins and come into my life. If you don't think I've changed because of Christ living in my life, just ask my wife. She tried to change me a thousand times and couldn't. The living Christ changed me in an instant and she has seen the evidence of Christ in me. Ask Jesus into your life and you too will know He's alive. Pick up the book "The Case for Christ" by Lee Strobel if you want to study more on this subject.

Kingdom of God

How long does it take for something to fall into disrepair? The worst thing that can happen to a house or a car is to not use it. The facts are that everything on this planet needs to be maintained in order to look and operate the way it was designed. There was a man who owned a farm. He invited a friend to visit him and was showing him around his pride and joy. He pointed out the fresh paint job on the barn and said, "Me and God did that." He drove his friend out to where his garden was growing in perfect rows with a mega harvest on every stalk. Again he said, "Me and God planted this crop. He brought his friend into the main house and began to brag on its impeccable condition. "Me and God did this." He beamed. The exasperated friend finally said, "You keep taking credit for everything you are showing me as if God needed your help." The proud owner replied, "You should have seen this place when God had it by Himself!"

The Kingdom of God has been entrusted to the people of God to maintain and see that its kept in good order. Jesus transferred the day to day business of the Kingdom to the church when He turned the keys of the Kingdom over the Peter. "I will give you the keys of the kingdom of heaven; whatever you bind on earth will be bound in heaven, and whatever you loose on earth will be loosed in heaven." (Matthew 16:19, NIV) We have a responsibility to care for the sick and poor. We have a duty to make sure the Scriptures are not compromised. We have the privilege of bringing the Good News of Jesus and His great Salvation to the entire world.

I have a question for you. How are we doing the job that's been entrusted to us? I believe if we look around we would see the place could use a little sprucing up. Church denominations are diminishing in huge numbers. The sick are not being prayed for so that they might be healed. The poor are dependent on the government. The hopeless and despondent have still not heard that Jesus loves them. What are you doing to care for the Kingdom of God? Are you waiting for someone else to do the job? When Jesus returns will He say to you, "Well done good and faithful servant?" It's way past time for all of us to be about our Father's business.

Leadership

"Lead, follow, or get out of the way!" was the heading on a large poster I used to have hanging on my office wall. The artwork on the poster showed a host of geese with their heads stretched high, as if to see above the crowd, each trying to move in different directions. It was a subliminal message to all who came into my sacred den to seek my advice or tell me what to do, that I understood the principles of leadership.

Jesus was a great leader. Those who followed Him knew it right away because He said, "Follow me." There were actually three groups of people who walked in Jesus' footsteps. First, there were the true believers who knew where Jesus was headed because they knew that He alone had the true message of life. In fact, one day when a portion of His band of followers walked away from Him, Jesus asked His inner circle if they wanted to leave too. Peter, a leader himself, who spoke for the remainder of the group, replied, "Lord, to whom shall we go? You have the words of eternal life." (John 6:68, NIV) A valuable element of leadership is garnered from this incident. Not everyone will stick with a leader when things get tough.

The second group of followers are those who will follow anyone because they don't know where to go and they don't know the truth. Jim Jones has become a synonym for these sheep who carelessly "baa baa" their way to the Kool-Aid stand. Every true leader must understand that all those who follow them are not committed to the truth and will take off to skip behind the next voice they hear.

The third group of followers are those who are just passing by on their way to nowhere in particular. They have their heads up in the constantly reshaping fluffy clouds, looking for those things that make them happy for a fleeting moment. They have no desire to know the truth. Jesus encountered these in His life and identified them as those who were looking for the next free meal of fish and bread. Effective leaders must understand that the crowds behind them may not have bought into their message and may leave at any time to follow another pleasant voice.

How would you describe the flock that is following your leadership? Those who lead in the pathway of the Gospel must understand that their devotees may not be followers of Christ but just enthusiasts of you. Following you is not enough. Those who follow you must first follow Christ or they will soon wander away to the next leader who will tickle their ears. A leader in the Kingdom of God needs to tirelessly remind their followers that Christ is at the head of the crowd. Lift them on your shoulders so that they always see Him. When they are following Him they will follow you.

Learning To Live

Have you ever tried to teach a child how to do something, like using a fork to eat their food, or tying their shoes? In their excitement to accomplish this new task, they grab the eating utensil from you, make feeble attempts at putting the food into their mouths, and end up with a mess. Or they end up with shoelaces that are untidy knots instead of neatly arranged bows. It's not their willingness that is causing the problem, but their sense of believing they can do it by themselves that hinders them. We, like children, carry this trait of self-reliance into our Christian lives.

So often we experience frustration and failure in our lives because we try to accomplish the task of living our lives without the assistance of God. We discard the gentle instructions of the Good Shepherd, and find ourselves wandering in the desert instead of reclining by the still waters. Jesus said it this way, "Walk with me and work with me —watch how I do it. Learn the unforced rhythms of grace. I won't lay anything heavy or ill-fitting on you. Keep company with me and you'll learn to live freely and lightly."" (Matthew 11:29–30, MSG) What a glorious difference when we learn how to live from Him. His promise is that we don't have to do it alone. His voice will give us instructions. His hands will cover ours and show us how to use our untrained skills. He will teach us in such a way, that we can live in confidence, knowing the right way to live.

The last part of the above scripture states we can learn to live life "freely and lightly." How different is that description from the way you are experiencing life today? Are you being ruled by failure? Fear? Doubt? Peter, the great Apostle, was able to walk on water when he kept his eyes on Jesus. When he concentrated on himself and his circumstances he began to sink. Today, why not lift your eyes to Jesus, and put your hands in His hands, so He can guide you through life, and turn your defeats into delights.

Liberty Has a Price

The cost of freedom is very high for those who step up to pay the price. I was watching a movie recently that recounted the ten days prior to the invasion of allied troops into Europe during World War II. The focus of the movie was the commander of all allied troops in Europe, General Dwight Eisenhower. The movie described the presentation of Project Overlord, as the invasion was code named, to the King of England and Prime Minister Winston Churchill. The King asked about the casualties they could expect as they landed on the German fortified beaches of France. General Eisenhower replied they would be very high. The air invasion alone estimated the loss of life at upwards of seventy percent.

The General then went on to tell of how as a young man he had visited Europe and saw all its beauty and wonder. He had pondered how he wished other American young men, most of whose ancestry was in Europe, could experience what he was seeing. He said, "Your Majesty, I never dreamed that millions of young American men would come to liberate Europe." He went on to say, that Americans were willing to leave the safety of America to wage war in order to insure that oppressed people could be free. "Many will die here to insure freedom for people they don't even know." When Eisenhower paused and lowered his head, feeling the burden of the task before him, the King stood up and began to clap his hands. Churchill stood and joined him as everyone in the room rose and a crescendo of applause filled that secret meeting room.

There are white stone crosses and Star of David monuments around the world that testify to the bravery, valor, dedication and cost of freedom paid by the American military. I think it fitting that the markers over their graves also speak of the God of King David and our Savior, Jesus, who gave His life for all mankind at Calvary. May each hero who purchased our freedom rest in peace for all eternity.

There is no way to repay the families who suffered such loss to preserve and defend freedom in places whose names I don't even know. In my hometown, I know a man whose father never returned from WWII. I stop by each Memorial Day and thank him for the sacrifice his family made so I could be free. This Memorial Day we should each take time to thank God for our freedom and those who secured and preserved it.

Life is a Vapor

Picture scrapbooks are a fountain of fond memories for us. They record vacations, baby's first steps, weddings and other festive occasions. With the advent of computers that hold our digital pictures, our scrapbooks are being neglected and the memories forgotten. I recently dug out the boxes of pictures from my parents and, with the help of my daughter, scanned them into my computer. What a rush of memories. Were we ever that young? That skinny? Had that much hair? Who are those people?

It occurred to me as I strolled down memory lane that life goes by way too fast. My parents who were once so young have left this life and inherited eternal life. My children now have children whose digital pictures are now filling cyber scrapbooks. It will be no time at all when they will look at those pictures and say, "What was I doing that was so important, that life slipped by me so fast?"

The bible says that all our days are numbered. In other words, there are a limited number of days that we all have to live. Each day is priceless and worth more than all the riches of the world. James wrote in the bible, "Today—at the latest, tomorrow—we're off to such and such a city for the year. We're going to start a business and make a lot of money." You don't know the first thing about tomorrow. You're nothing but a wisp of fog, catching a brief bit of sun before disappearing." (James 4:13-14, MSG) Wow, "a wisp of fog!" James is saying we had better live today before it disappears into a fading memory.

Play with your kids. Hug your spouse. Drink a cup of coffee with a friend. Laugh. Go on an adventure. Visit your parents. Pray. Go to church. Have fun while you're able to do it. Jesus came to give us an abundant life. Don't throw away your life by ignoring it. Why not break out those scrapbooks, gather the family together, and enjoy a trip down memory lane? It will be time well spent.

Loneliness

I'm an only child. Now if you have siblings you have no idea what it means to be an only child. It has its benefits and detriments. Growing up I could never blame anyone else for what I'd just done. I just had to stand there and take the well-deserved punishment for my infraction of the rules. But, when there was a box of candy in the house, I didn't have to share it, or fight with a hostile brother or sister over the last piece. I just popped it in my mouth and relished the moment.

Elvis Presley was an only child. So were Brook Shields, Frank Sinatra, Joe Montana, Leonardo de Vinci and a host of other mostly normal people. The most famous only child to grace our planet was Jesus. Now He had some half brothers and sisters but that's a theological argument for another time. So where am I going with this unimportant only child nonsense? Its about feeling alone most of your life. God never wanted us to be alone. He created Adam and said it wasn't good for Him to be alone. One of Adams first instructions was to multiply.

The bible tells us we are not alone even when we think we are. I really like the place in the Twenty-Third Psalm where God describes the intimate relationship He has with His people. "Even though I walk through the valley of the shadow of death, I will fear no evil, for you are with me; your rod and your staff, they comfort me." (Psalms 23:4, NIV) He is with me. His rod, which is a weapon to ward off predators, is in His hands. His staff, a tool to guide me and yank me away from precarious places, is by His side. He's got me covered. I preached a sermon on this awhile back and coined the phrase, "I'm not alone and I'm not afraid." Pretty good don't you think?

You see, only children often feel alone. But so do people from large families. Be encouraged today. Try repeating, "I'm not alone and I'm not afraid." to yourself until you experience the peace that happens when you are aware that Jesus is right beside you. Go ahead and do it! No one will hear but you and Jesus.

Long Life

I just saw a study done around the world to discover why some people in some places live an average of about 100 years. That's right there are a few places on earth where people live 20 years or so longer than anywhere else. A few of the things that contribute to their longevity are: an active lifestyle even at 100 plus; a good diet with lots of veggies; a moderate consumption of alcoholic beverages; a day of rest each week; great family values; devoted religious faith life.

When I saw that, I immediately thought of the many instructions in the bible given by God: Those who don't work don't eat; Eat lots of plant food and avoid shellfish and some meats; A little wine is good for your stomach; The seventh day is a day of rest; Honor your father and mother and obey them; Love God with all your being. Wow! We could conclude that following the admonitions of the scriptures could add years to your life. Who woulda thunk it?

But wait! There's more than a long life on earth that awaits those who follow the teachings of the bible. God promises a good life here and eternal life when you finally die, whatever your age. Jesus said it this way: "The thief does not come except to steal, and to kill, and to destroy. I have come that they may have life, and that they may have *it* more abundantly." (John 10:10, NKJ, emphasis mine) The thief of life is the devil and all his lies that deceive people into believing there is no God, and if there is, he's a weak cruel being that doesn't really care about you. "And eternal life?" he quips. "When you die you die and its back to the dust of the earth."

The truth is that those who truly know God understand that He is attentive to all your needs. He constantly thinks about you. He loves you so much that He sent His Son to die for your sins and bestow on you an abundant life here, and eternal life after death. Maybe you should change the way you think about God. He offers quite a life.

Love and Marriage

June is here and the wedding dresses are flying off the racks. It seems that June nuptials began with the Italians or more specifically the Romans. The Romans had a marriage goddess named Juno (they had a god for everything) so June became a popular month to get married. Juno has drifted off into the ash can of history but June weddings still persist. I've performed a lot of June weddings, but the major reason brides pick June is tradition. The biggest tradition in June weddings is declaring of eternal love and union "until death do us part." Based on the percentages of June weddings that end up in divorce it seems death has been redefined as "until we fall out of love," which brings me to the subject I have in mind. What is love?

Most Christian weddings define love by reading the quintessential definition found in the bible. "Love is patient, love is kind. It does not envy, it does not boast, it is not proud. It does not dishonor others, it is not self-seeking, it is not easily angered, it keeps no record of wrongs. Love does not delight in evil but rejoices with the truth. It always protects, always trusts, always hopes, and always perseveres. Love never fails." (1 Corinthians 13:4-8, NIV) Wow! If love is all these things, and it ends with the definitive statement "Love never fails," how come marriages fail when brides and grooms "fall out of love?" I'll tell you why. Because love is not enough!

Marriages fail because marriage is like a hot bathtub you get into, and when the water cools, you get out of the tub. And love always cools. The source of an eternal flame that can keep a marriage hot is by loving and serving God and each other. Your commitment to keep the vows you made before God and your spouse have to go deeper than mere love. The bedrock of marriage is Christ the Rock. Being committed to Him and having a firm determination to do everything to make sure your spouse is well cared for, protected, and honored until death, not until love wanes. Look back at the definition of love in this article and you will discover that love is something you do, not something you feel. So, how are you "doing" love?

Mardi Gras and Sin

Ah, the sound of silence. Mardi Gras is over at last. The floats are parked in their warehouses. The costumes are hung in the back of the closet. The last remnant of Ash Wednesday ashes has been washed away. Gause Boulevard in my town is free from all traffic congestion and life is back to normal.

And there you have it. Life after Carnival. I always find it strange that people are given license to go wild before Mardi Gras, and then become sweet religious saints afterward. I have searched my bible and can't find any hint of a suggestion that we can be free to sin and then turn on our halos, as if the uncomely behavior was okay with God.

I suppose the pre and post Mardi Gras behavior is like following the Law, as given by Moses. We break the Law, bring a sacrifice to the Temple, ask for forgiveness and go back and break the Law again.

This cycle of behavior by mankind leads to spiritual insanity. Then at the end of our lives we "hope" somehow God will turn the other way and let us into heaven. Not! The only people who get into heaven are perfect people. That fact gives us a perfect dilemma because no one is perfect. "What are we to do," you might ask?

God understood our problem and showered the earth with Grace. Grace says that God has wiped away every sin you ever committed when Christ died on the Cross. He became sin!. All He asks is that you believe that Jesus died on the cross for you and ask Him into your life to help you live every day according to His perfect plan. Some say that's not fair and that we are responsible for our sins and need to pay for them. If you believe that, you are in big trouble and will ride on an eternal float in an eternal parade to an eternal hell. What God offers is not fair. That's why He called it Grace. "For it is by grace you have been saved, through faith—and this is not from yourselves, it is the gift of God— not by works, so that no one can boast." (Ephesians 2:8-9, NIV)

Marriage and Love

"How do I love thee? Let me count the ways. I love thee to the depth and breadth and height My soul can reach…" wrote Elizabeth Barrett Browning. When wives ask men if they love them, they might answer, "How do I love thee? Let me show you the ways. I go to work every day, I make sure we have money to pay the bills, I dress up when your parents visit us and I fixed the dishwasher last year. Ain't that love?"

God says that a man should love his wife as Christ loves the church. Holy cow! Who can love that much? And what about the standards for wives? Wives are to submit to their husbands as they submit themselves to the Lord. Most of the time when these passages of scripture come up, they are explained away as stuff they had to do back-in-the-day, which is no longer relevant to modern society. Perhaps that's why we have so many unhappy marriages and so many divorces.

Is it possible to follow the scriptural instructions for husbands and wives today? How would a woman feel if her husband loved her as Christ loved the church? How would a man respond if his wife recognized him as the leader of the family and submitted to him? I can tell you from experience helping troubled marriages that if you follow these instructions from God it will transform the entire family. When husbands become attentive, it makes a woman feel beautiful and wanted again. The bad emotions of insecurity wives have inside them melt away in the warmth of the love of their husbands. When wives put down the weight of leading the family, and pass that heavy responsibility to their husbands, men rise up and shoulder the task with ease, because God ordained that they should carry the load for their families. They begin to walk upright with godly pride.

"A man will leave his father and mother and be united to his wife, and the two will become one flesh." (Ephesians 5:31, NIV) God's plan revolves around following His instructions, because by doing so, husbands and wives draw closer together as one.

God put in men the ability to lift the loads of life for their families. He put in women the ability to help their husbands be what God always intended they should be. Husbands and wives need each other, and they are fully equipped to create an environment of love and respect that fosters a home filled with love and happiness. When God's plan is put into action and you ask your spouse, "How do you love me?" They might respond, "Do you have a couple of hours so I can explain how much you mean to me?"

Memorial Day

A missionary friend of mine was assigned to the Micronesian Islands in the South Pacific. He was close enough to the island of Iwo Jima that he was able to take his relatively small boat and travel to this famous World War II battleground where so many Americans were wounded and others gave their lives for our freedom. When he arrived at the deserted coral beach, he made his way up to the top of the mountain where the American flag was raised in victory. He found a monument there to commemorate the raising of the flag and the price paid in blood for that island so long ago. There was a brass plaque attached to it by four bolts that read: "Lest We Forget." Sadly, three of the bolts had rusted away and the memorial plaque was dangling by the remaining rusting bolt. To any visitor to the island, it would seem that the sign that was placed to insure we would never forget that place, was a reminder that the island and it's history were certainly forgotten.

Our nation has set aside the last Monday in May as the day that we remember those who gave everything for freedom. We've named it Memorial Day. A small remnant of patriots will place flags at military gravesides, along highways and other places to say, "Thank you, fallen ones, we remember." Yet, the vast majority of Americans will remember the fallen with hot dogs, cold beer and warm beaches. The sand covered ground from Europe, The Pacific, Iraq and Afghanistan won't be acknowledged or remembered. The blood spilled around the globe and soaked into the ground, for our freedom won't be memorialized. How sad. How disrespectful. How could they...

How about a new Memorial Day tradition? A tradition against forgetting. Let's take time this year to fall to our knees to pray and remember those who fell so we could pray. Let's pull out the pictures of forgotten heroes and show them to our children and grandchildren. Let's salute the American flag and recite that old pledge to the flag that still contains the phrase, "One nation under God, with liberty and justice for all." Let's do these things while we can. "Lest we Forget."

Mind of Christ

What do you think about when you're not thinking about anything? In other words, when your mind is in idle where does it gravitate? Let me explain what I'm asking. People who are worriers begin to think about things to worry about. People who are depressed look for things that depress them. People who are joyful are filled with joyful thoughts. Happy people think happy thoughts. The essence of who you are, determines in great part, what you will think about.

How do you change the way you think? That is a question that has filled more couches in more doctor's offices than there are fish in the sea. It's hard to get a person to alter their thought patterns. Doctors, in frustration, and because they have very few options, prescribe mind altering drugs. Those who don't trust doctors or can't afford them, self prescribe alcohol or illegal drugs to change the way they think. Most prescribed drugs or self-administered treatments put people into mental conditions where they can scarcely function in life.

Is there a better way to change the way you think? Yes! And the answer is so simple that most people never see it or reject it as sheer foolishness. The answer is that you need the mind of Christ. You see, the mind of Christ is perfect and healthy in every way, and when you have the mind of Christ, it alters the manner in which you think and evaluate the situations in life.

You receive the mind of Christ when you invite Him into your life and allow Him to rewire the way you think. His thoughts are helpful, wise, joyful, loving and filled with eternal hope for the future. "Finally, brothers, whatever is true, whatever is noble, whatever is right, whatever is pure, whatever is lovely, whatever is admirable—if anything is excellent or praiseworthy—think about such things." (Philippians 4:8, NIV) Your response may be "I can't do that because it won't work for me." I have a question for you. "How is what you are doing working for you?" If it's not, then why not give Jesus a chance? The truth is that at this very moment Jesus is thinking about you. He sees your situation and wants to help you. He is waiting for you to ask Him for help. "He is able to do far more abundantly beyond all that we ask or think, according to the power (Christ) that works within us." (Ephesians 3:20, NAS) He is ready and able to do more for you than you could ever ask or think that He could do. Think not? Think again!

Mother's Day

I never realized how vastly important Mother's Day was until the year after my mother died. It was always just part of life to buy a card or send flowers or take mom out to dinner. Hey it was Mother's Day and I wanted to let my mom know I loved and appreciated her. Then the realization hit me that I didn't need to buy her anything anymore. I had heard hundreds of times people say you had better pay attention to your mom while she's alive. When she's gone, you will miss her more than you know. They were right. But I have no regrets. I loved her and treated her as best I knew how as long as she was alive.

So what should you do if your mom is still alive? If I know your mom she is probably like most moms and cherishes those special days more than you realize. I know those Mother's Day cards are mushy and sentimental beyond belief, but moms love them! The cards use words that often times we are too timid to say out loud. "Thanks mom for being so kind and understanding," or "A mothers love is warm and gentle, generous and sentimental," or "A mothers love is precious in so many special ways." (Courtesy of Hallmark Cards) We don't normally speak to mom in those terms. Most often we just say, "I love ya mom" as we place a kiss on her cheek. But moms love to read those cards and cry when they do, shedding tears that gently fall between the fold of the card. I remember going through mom's things after she died and finding all the cards I had sent her through the years. Birthday and Mother's Day cards topped the list. They were more valuable to her than I ever realized.

So Mother's Day will be here tomorrow. If your mom's around let her know how much you love her and go buy her one of those mushy cards. You might find it again one day when you are going through her things. And if you take the time to read it, you will probably shed matching tears to hers that will drop and stain the card once more with tears of love. You will doubtless save those precious cards for yourself. I have.

Murder

What would Jesus say about the senseless murders in Arizona not so long ago? This is easy. He said it a long time ago through the prophet Moses. In fact, He didn't just say it, He chiseled it in stone with His finger. "Thou shall not kill." I think it's pretty clear that for a long time God has been against murder. Also remember that God was not pleased with Cain when he murdered Abel before the stone tablets were given.

I heard the question asked, "How could a good God allow a little nine year old girl to die and not stop it?" It seems a bit out of line to blame God for what a demon possessed, deranged, mad man did. How about let's ask a few questions from the enemies of God:

"Satan, why do you hate us so much that you do everything in your power to deceive, condemn and murder us?"

"Judges, why do you let bad men out of jail when their records show that they will commit crimes again?"

"Politicians, why do you say you are pro choice, knowing that a baby in its mother's womb will end up a bloody, dismembered heap in a medical trash basket?"

"Lawmakers, why did you take prayer and the bible out of our schools?"

I think there are lots of guilty people in society to blame other than God. He has chosen to let us choose the kind of society we want to live in. And sure enough we have created a world we can't live in. If we want to blame someone for what's wrong in America, when a beautiful nine year old girl lies lifeless on the streets of Tucson, we had best look in the mirror.

We have been silent while reckless people have stripped the moral standards of society from us. Pulpits have been silent as the moral fiber of our nation has been taken from us.

I believe that God is good and that He weeps over what we have done. His plan is to love and spend eternity with His creation. But men have rejected God and suffer the consequences we see every day in the news. Will God bring judgment upon a nation that rejects Him? There are examples of that happening in the bible in both the Old and New Testaments. However, there is a better way to change what's wrong with our world. Jesus gave us the blueprint when He departed planet earth. He said for us to go and bring the world to it's knees, not with brute force, but with the spiritual power of the Gospel. "Go ye therefore, and teach all nations, baptizing them in the name of the Father, and of the Son, and of the Holy Ghost: Teaching them to observe all things whatsoever I have commanded you: and, lo, I am with you alway, even unto the end of the world. Amen." (Matthew 28:19-20, KJV)

New Year's Resolutions

Whew... We made it through Christmas again. Sigh... Now we can all start feeling better. New Years is just a few days away and everything is going to be just fine. I like New Years because it gives us a chance to get a fresh run at life. We will have New Year's resolutions to keep that will revolutionize our lives. The diet! The Gym! The Budget! The resolve to change! Good-bye to the old and hello to the new! Its gonna be great!

Now I realize that most of us... no, all of us, broke our New Year's resolutions last year. But that was then and this is now. We're older. Wiser. Stronger. We can do it! But... can we??? From what I have seen each year, we have about as much chance of keeping the New Year's commitments as we have of winning the lottery. It's possible, but not probable. So why do we bother? Because, something inside of us wants our life to be better. It's a hope that is standard equipment in every son and daughter of Adam. We know we can do better. It's like a movie I saw with Jack Nicholson, when he kisses the girl at the end and does a lousy job. He looks at the girl with determination and says, "I know I can do better!" So he gave her another kiss that was worthy of an academy award as the sweet strains of music played and rolling credits ended the movie.

You can do better! But you need help. All our resolutions are flawed behavior modifications that never work. God in His wisdom gave us a behavior barometer that proves we can't alter our behavior very well. He had Moses chisel the Ten Commandments into stone and presented them to us. (I think it was New Year's Day, back-in-the-day.) And everyone, from Moses to us, has broken them so many times that the stone has been pulverized into dust.

Then God gave us a better way to change. He gave us His only begotten Son, Jesus, to save us from our flawed behavior. He said if we would believe in Jesus we would get a permanent New Beginning. Jesus referred to it as being born again. St. Paul put it this way: "Whoever is a believer in Christ is a new creation. The old way of living has disappeared. A new way of living has come into existence." (2 Corinthians 5:17, GWT) You see, as a believer in Christ, He resides inside of you and can reform your actions according to His perfect plan for your life. How about this New Year you resolve to turn your life over to Him and see what a difference He can make? Happy New Year!

Noah and the Ark

The phone rings and the call gives you the news that will change your life forever. Your mind races with outrageous thoughts about the subject of the call. Those thoughts run the spectrum of unbelief, fear, and hopelessness. What did you do wrong to deserve this? Then the big blame-it-on-God thoughts come to your mind. Why doesn't God do something to stop the flood of anguish you are going through?

Right after Katrina ravished the Gulf Coast, a CD was released to help the people who were going through so much. One of the songs was a dialogue with God that said, "I thought it would be over by now. But it's still raining." Sometimes it rains for the preverbal 40 days. And then it really starts to rain hard. What are you supposed to do in a rainstorm? According to the bible you're supposed to build an ark.

A few facts about the ark. (1) God saw Noah's plight and the scripture says "Noah found grace in the eyes of the Lord." (2) God told Noah to build something he had never seen before – the ark. (3) Building something to carry you through the flood takes time and effort. (4) God saved Noah and his family from the flood in the ark. So how does this apply to your rainstorm?

God sees you and cares about you and is willing to intervene in your life. But it won't be the way you think it will be. God could have stopped the rain, but he had Noah participate in the solution by building the ark. Ask God what would He have you do, and then do it! He may tell you to pray. He may tell you to trust Him. He may tell you that His grace is sufficient to carry you through. I don't know what He will tell you and you won't either until you ask. The promise of God is that those who seek Him "will" find Him. "For I know the plans I have for you," says the LORD. "They are plans for good and not for disaster, to give you a future and a hope. In those days when you pray, I will listen." (Jeremiah 29:11-12, NLT)

You might say that prayer is just a canned answer to your situation. You prayed and nothing changed. I say, "Keep praying until God answers." If you're drowning, what are your options? If you had the power to fix your situation, you would. But you can't. I believe Noah doubted God with every nail he hammered to build the ark. He could have stopped anywhere along the way. But he didn't, and the rest, as they say, is history. Keep hammering on heaven's door. You need an ark. And the only way to get plans for an ark to save you are the prayers you pray.

Power

Jesus, as He was about to ascend into heaven, told His disciples not to go anywhere until they received the power He had promised them. I think it's thought provoking that He said the church would need power. The Greek word that is translated, as "power" is the word from which we derive the two English words, dynamite and dynamo. So, Jesus said the church would need power that could explode and blow things up, and power that could generate energy. In other words, power to destroy and power to sustain.

Obviously Jesus was not describing physical weapons or machinery but spiritual weapons. "The weapons we fight with are not the weapons of the world. On the contrary, they have divine power to demolish strongholds. We demolish arguments and every pretension that sets itself up against the knowledge of

God, and we take captive every thought to make it obedient to Christ." (2 Corinthians 10:4-5, NIV) There are strongholds of evil on this earth that can only be defeated by the spiritual weapons provided by God to the church. The world is filled with evil that inhabits men and drives them to exhibit bizarre insane behavior. The massacre in Columbine, Colorado some time back that killed so many children, is an example of such evil. Many voices declare we need more laws to stop evil. The bible would disagree. What we need is the power to tear down the evil strongholds.

The thoughts of men need to be under the sustaining power of God. That power can change the way men think and thus change the way they behave. The scripture states that there is a way of thinking that seems right to men but that method of thinking leads to death. The only sanity in creation is the mind of Christ. "For, "Who can know the LORD's thoughts? Who knows enough to teach him?" But we understand these things, for we have the mind of Christ." (1 Corinthians 2:16, NLT) Men who have the mind of Christ through faith in Him can change the world and drive out evil thoughts and imaginations by His dynamic power.

We need a major change in America, our churches and our homes. God can initiate this change. The fuse that ignites and releases the power of God is the Name of Jesus. The whole world was turned upside down when the power of God fell on the church in the book of Acts. That power is still available today to all who receive Christ and ask for the gift of the Holy Spirit.

Praise to God

How many things have gone wrong this week? I'll bet you can remember a bunch. How many things have gone right? Hmmm... Having trouble remembering the good events? Why is it that we can name our troubles without hesitation and have to stop and reach into our memory banks to remember the good? Could it be we have an expectation that life should be on a constant yellow-brick-road with blue birds singing and cloudless skies?

We have the nasty habit of blaming God for whatever goes wrong and seldom, if ever, think about Him on the good days. God, on any given day, is working to insure your life is good. He shuffles life's occurrences like pieces of a puzzle to create a beautiful life for you. St. Paul put it this way, "And we know that God causes everything to work together for the good of those who love God and are called according to his purpose for them." (Romans 8:28, NLT)

For some unexplainable reason, we rush to judgment against God when circumstances don't go the way we want them to go, and we fail to acknowledge God when He showers us with blessings. We treat God as if He was the government and we are entitled to blessings. Look at what God said about this self-centered mindset, "I took care of you, took care of all your needs, gave you everything you needed. You were spoiled. You thought you didn't need me. You forgot me." (Hosea 13:6, MSG)

You have so much to be grateful for you should spend a portion of every day just thanking God. If you are reading this, you can thank God for the ability to read. If you are not in the hospital, thank Him for your health. If you can see, taste, smell, walk, speak, think, remember, love, are loved and know God, your voice should be a trumpet of praise sounding in the hallways of heaven, telling all creation how good Father is to you. "This is the day the LORD has made. We/I will rejoice and be glad in it." (Psalms 118:24, NLT) Now, don't you feel better about today with praise rising up from your heart?

Prayer

"Rome wasn't built in a day." At least that's what we say. We don't really care about Rome but we recognize that sometimes things take time to complete. Nine months for a baby. Five years to complete the new Twin Spans bridge across Lake Pontchartrain. A couple of days or weeks for a hurricane to form in the ocean and roll onshore. What about things that happen in an instant? Tornados. You're fired! Accidents. We all agree that we should pray, but sometimes the only prayer you have time for is a frantic "Help me Jesus!" So how does this prayer thing work?

The word most commonly used in the bible for prayer is derived from a combination of two words: nearness and wills. Whenever we are dealing with Rome-wasn't-built-in-a-day issues, we can't rush into His presence like an out of breath child wanting a piece of candy. The Psalms give us a picture of this nearness concept. "Enter his gates with thanksgiving; go into his courts with praise. Give thanks to him and praise his name." (Psalms 100:4, NIV) We enter God's presence and thank Him and praise Him before we ask Him.

The second part of prayer is when we ask God about what He believes is best for us. And we bend our will to match His will. Jesus demonstrated prayer when He went to the Garden of Gethsemane and prayed, "Father, if you are willing, please take this cup of suffering away from me. Yet I want your will to be done, not mine." (Luke 22:42, NIV) Do you see it? "Your will be done, not mine." The mindset I most often try to achieve when I'm bringing my request to God is – ambivalence. I'm ready to praise God if I get a new car or if I don't. I'm ready to praise God if I get healed or if I don't. I acknowledge that His will for me is always better than my will for me.

So there you have it. When you pray, get close to God and be willing to go with His plan for your life. However, there will be situations when you won't have time for this lengthy method of prayer. If you're about to get in a car wreck, and flip over the side of the new Twin Spans into the murky waters of Lake Pontchartrain, just shout out "Help me Jesus!" God's big enough to know what to do in an emergency. He's the original EMT.

Pre-Incarnate Christ

Did you know that the pre-incarnate Christ appeared to people before He was born in Bethlehem's crib? It takes a bit of study to find all such appearances, but the ones that most theologians agree on, are when He appeared to Isaiah, Hagar, Abraham, Jacob and Joshua. At these appearances He is often thought to be an angel but then the realization set in and they all proclaimed that they were in the presence of the Lord.

The one meeting that most intrigues me is when Jacob encountered the pre-incarnate Jesus. Jacob was on his way back to his family after he had deceived his brother and run away. He was a bit fearful at what kind of reception he would receive and spent a night alone in prayer. During that prayer time a man appeared and began to wrestle with him until the morning broke forth on a new day. The man could not get away from Jacob so in the struggle he touched Jacob's hip and knocked it out of its socket. Still, Jacob would not relent and told the man he would not let him go until he blessed him. The man finally agreed and actually told Jacob that from that day forward his name was changed to Israel. Jacob said, "It is because I saw God face to face, and yet my life was spared." (Genesis 32:30, NIV)

The whole world knows about Israel but not many know this account of how Jacob received this name that even to this day, is still the name of his nation. I believe for the rest of his life when people asked him about his name change and why he walked with a limp, he related this awesome night when he saw God who was the Christ to come.

Have you ever had an experience with God that has changed you for your entire life? Do people see such a change in you that they ask what happened to change the way you walk through life? Everyone needs an encounter with Jesus. He has the ability to touch you in such a way that you are never the same again. If you have never had a life changing encounter with Jesus, why not get alone with Him and refuse to leave His presence until He touches you in such a way that you will never be the same again. Who knows? He might even give you a new name. But one thing He will do for sure, is write your name in His book, "The Lamb's Book of Life."

Proof of the Resurrection

I don't know the exact number but there is a vast amount of people around the globe who don't believe in God. According to a Gallup poll conducted in June of 2012, 59% of the world population define themselves as being religious. Another poll says that 32% of the world's population is Christian. I don't trust polls all that much so I would not put much "faith" in those numbers. But I know of a poll that is 100% accurate. Everyone who has died believes in God. Here on earth there are a lot of opinions but when you die the only poll that counts is God's when He asks if you believe now.

There was a very large debate some time back between an atheist and a Christian theologian. At the end of the debate over 80% of the people acknowledged that the debate persuaded them that God exists. What was so compelling was that Dr. William Craig defended the resurrection with common sense. William Craig saw that the only thing that makes sense, after looking at all the evidence for and against the resurrection, is that Christ is alive!

Paul wrote to the Corinthians about the Resurrection, "And if Christ has not been raised, then your faith is useless and you are still guilty of your sins. In that case, all who have died believing in Christ are lost! And if our hope in Christ is only for this life, we are more to be pitied than anyone in the world." (1 Corinthians 15:17-19, NLT) Paul was not afraid to debate the case that God exists and that Jesus is alive. No event in all history has been investigated more than the missing body of Jesus. His grave was empty then and it remains empty today. The Romans with all their resources could not find the body. The Jews, who were desperate to recover it, could not find it. Even Jesus' disciples were dumbstruck and confused because the body was not where they put it. "He appeared to Peter, and then to the Twelve. After that, he appeared to more than five hundred of the brothers at the same time, most of whom are still living, though some have fallen asleep. Then he appeared to James, then to all the apostles, and last of all he appeared to me also." (1 Corinthians 15:5-8, NIV) That's evidence that would even persuade the United States Supreme Court. Friends, Jesus is alive! You may elect to reject that provable fact today, but one day, when you die, you'll join the 100% who know by sight what Christians know by faith. Don't wait until it's too late.

Pure Grace

A fellow pastor and friend of mine, Clark Whitten, wrote his first book and titled it "Pure Grace." I had one of the biggest laughs as I read Clark's statement about the freedom Christ has imparted to those who are Believers. He wrote in part on page 20: "Christians are truly free. We are free to laugh or cry, read a novel or the Bible, eat meat offered to idols or avoid it, drink wine or water, smoke or chew, get fat or fit, attend church or stay home, tithe or give nothing – all without condemnation from God." I told my wife between gulps of air and laughter, "Pastor Clark has set the battle lines between Law and Grace. Most pastors will throw this book in the trash and start preaching against it."

Are we truly that free in Christ? Is it true God does not get steamed and start throwing stones at us because we don't follow the rules? Who made up these rules anyway? Sad to say most of the "expected" behavior placed on the shoulders of

Believers came from control freak pastors who want to make sure you follow their guidelines. They cloak their desire to control you by blaming the rules on God. They say, "God is watching and if you break the rules He's gonna get you!" No wonder our churches are half empty and the percentage of people who claim to be Christians has fallen to alarmingly low numbers.

Christ came to set us free from foolish rules so we could worship Him in spirit and truth. Look at what He said to the rule makers of His day: "And you experts in the law, woe to you, because you load people down with burdens they can hardly carry, and you yourselves will not lift one finger to help them." (Luke 11:46, NIV)

Are Pastor Clark, me and Jesus saying you can do whatever you want and God doesn't care? No! We're saying stop worrying about senseless unbiblical man made rules and start listening to the voice of Jesus. He will lead you in the way you should go and teach you what you should and should not do. We are to be followers of Christ. What more is there? Jesus said, "Follow Me." By the way, I highly recommend Clark's book to anyone who wants to find out what Pure Grace is all about.

Refreshing

Those of us who live in the Deep South each year feel our lives being refreshed by the cool dry air of an October cold front passing by. The hot sweaty days of summer begin to fade and we can brave the outdoors and enjoy ourselves once again. We can finally break out those sweaters and coats we placed in mothballs last spring.

Not only do our bodies need refreshing but also our souls. How often has a visit by a friend refreshed you? Perhaps an unexpected card from an old school chum. Just the sight of a child playing on a swing, giggling with a high-pitched laugh, can cause your entire being to relax.

I find quiet peace for my soul in the Psalms. Word pictures like Psalms 23 where it says, "He leads me beside still waters, He restores my soul…" When I take a moment to reflect on this, allowing my imagination to create a peaceful lake with a gentle breeze ruffling the waters, it causes my breathing to relax and my daily anxiety to drift away. I become aware of God's presence with me in Psalm 139 as it says, "How precious to me are your thoughts, God! How vast is the sum of them! Were I to count them, they would outnumber the grains of sand—" (Psalms 139:17-18, NIV) Can you imagine how many times God is thinking about you? We can't count the grains of sand in an hourglass and God's thoughts of you outnumber the grains of sand on the entire earth.

Psalm 1 informs us that those who spend time mediating about God will be continually refreshed, fruitful and prosperous. "They are like trees planted along the riverbank, bearing fruit each season. Their leaves never wither, and they prosper in all they do." (Psalms 1:3, NLT) God in His divine wisdom had these Psalms written and preserved for us, so we could be encouraged and find much needed rest. Why not pick up your bible, step outside with a hot cup of coffee and let your soul soar on the words of the Psalms.

Rejoice

When was the last time you had fun being a Christian? The Chaplin of Bourbon Street in New Orleans, Bob Harrington, used to say, "It's fun being saved!" Now, the glass-is-half-empty crowd will say, you don't have to have fun to be Christian. I agree. If you are a Christian who is being persecuted and facing a den of lions, you might not be laughing out loud. But Daniel seemed to get a good night's sleep when he was in the lion's den. Paul and Silas were able to sing and worship God when they were in the prison. "And at midnight Paul and Silas prayed, and sang praises unto God: and the prisoners heard them." (Acts 16:25, KJV)

I think sometimes we take life too seriously, and don't take the promises of God seriously enough. Sure, we have situations that require us to stop and catch out breath. But as Christians, if we can't laugh we ought to a least be able to rejoice.

Last week, I was preaching a sermon from Romans 8:1 that states, "Therefore, there is now no condemnation to those who are in Christ Jesus." That's good news! In the midst of all the bad news that floods our lives we need some good news. It's hard to feel bad when you are shouting praise to God for His marvelous grace.

Paul started Romans 8 with the word "Therefore" for a reason. In the last part of chapter 7, he opens his life to us and states that he is not always a happy camper. He confesses that he is helpless dealing with life. But in verse 7:25 he declares that Jesus is his only help. You can almost hear Paul shout, THEREFORE, THERE IS NOW NO CONDEMNATION…" Paul took seriously the promises of God, and in the middle of all that went wrong, he knew God was not angry with him.

Dear friends, the most important truth in your life is that God is not <u>NOW</u> condemning you. No matter what other horrible events may be crashing down on you, God is with you and He is on your side. Christ has dealt with all of your sins: past, present and future. No wonder Paul rejoiced even when he was in the darkest, dirtiest and most depressing place on the planet. The more he sang and praised God the better he felt. Try repeating Romans 8:1 out loud over and over until your heart begins to lift, your tears dry up and the only sound you hear is your voice worshiping God. You won't understand how this works until you try it.

Rest and Thanks

How's the New Year going? In typical New Orleans style, the old year is forgotten. The New Year is forgotten. Everyone is rushing to the future. Sugar Bowl. BCS playoff. Super Bowl. Mardi Gras. On and on it goes. Give me a break! How about an annual after-the-New-Year celebration of the "I'm Doing Nothing Bowl?"

The bible speaks of rest. There are lots of scriptures that say, "wait." What's the rush? Where are we going? The only way off this celestial ball named Earth, is by space ship or coffin. I'm not ready for either one. But I do need some rest.

Actually Jesus addressed this treadmill issue when He said, "Walk with me and work with me—watch how I do it. Learn the unforced rhythms of grace. I won't lay anything heavy or ill-fitting on you. Keep company with me and you'll learn to live freely and lightly." (Matthew 11:29-30, MSG) How cool is that? The way we get some rest is to align our lives with Christ. He's got it all under control. No more running hither and yon trying to get some joy out of life that we think will settle us down. We can learn about resting from Him.

Today, I was up early before sunrise and sitting before the fireplace thinking about God. The house was quiet. I was in the dark except for the flickering fire. I could breath easy. No rush. The cell phone was in another room. Peace… I could feel it way deep inside. I sat there for about an hour just enjoying a break thinking about and hearing in my heart from God. After about an hour I went into another part of the house that faces the east. There it was! The dawn of a new day! The darkness was being crowded out by the blue and orange hues of the sun. The first thought I had was, "God, what a majestic day you have created." I think I heard Him say, "Thank you."

Take a break and enjoy the day. Slow everything down. Rest with Him. Give God thanks for your life. Who knows, you might hear Him say, "Thanks for noticing all the wonderful things I'm doing for you."

Revival

Back in the ancient days when I first started attending church, I met a really on-fire man of God. He told me an interesting story. He said that whenever he introduced someone to Jesus, and they prayed and asked Him into their lives, that he did his best to keep them from going to church. He said he needed time to teach the new convert how to be a Christian. He went on to say that he wanted the new believer to pray, share his faith, study his bible and give financially. He felt that most churches didn't teach those principles, and therefore most people in the pews didn't practice them. I thought that was a cold and hard view of the church.

Here I am almost 40 years later and I think that guy might have been right. Not that we do those thing to curry favor with God, but they should be a natural fruit of the life of Christ in us. Most churches have a passive attitude toward Christianity. This seems out of character, especially here in America, since all of society seems bent on being the best. We love the fastest, strongest, loveliest, and best of everything. Hence, the popularity of the entertainment world's TV shows like American Idol, Dancing with the Stars, Top Shot, and game shows of every variety. Not to mention sports mania. My question is, "Why doesn't our excitement to side with winners translate into the church community?"

I believe that churches should be the most exciting places in town. There should be shouts of praise because someone asked Christ into their lives. Jubilation should be everywhere because a sick person was healed. Someone should be overjoyed as they rush to write their tithe and offering check. How about so much excitement that people on the outside are rushing in so they can get a seat before the church fills up? And what about a host of sinners asking if they could join you in your church?

When was the last time you went to church and everybody was excited about what Christ was doing in his or her lives? When has someone shouted during a sermon? "You go preacher!" Really, when you think about it, most churches are… well I hate to use the word… dead. There was a church in our town that had signs on the wall in bold letters that said,

"SILENCE." Maybe we don't need a revival in church but a resurrection.

You might say, "Pastor Morris, we don't do church like that anymore." Maybe it's time to start. Take a look around. The economy is in the tank. Jobs are non-existent. Murder, rape, robbery and sexual immorality are rampant. The Governor of New York won't even let ministers participate in the 9/11 dedication of the memorial because he thinks it would be "inappropriate." If the church is not excited about Christ, I assure you the world won't be either. When you attend church this Sunday, why not start a cheer for Jesus? Who knows? You might see a miracle and the dead might come back to life. Or you might be asked to leave.

Sacrifice

There is a word in our American vocabulary that we use almost daily. It's an unusual word and one that you would think would be used sparingly. The word is sacrifice. Its Latin origin is steeped in the imagery of Christ's sacrifice over two thousand years ago. Our use of this word ranges from a sacrifice play in baseball, to the stern voice of a parent to a child, explaining how much they sacrificed to put unappreciated food on the table.

The bible uses the word sacrifice almost four hundred times centered on the Temple and the animals that were sacrificed in an attempt to deal with sin. Back in the day when you committed some sin, you had to bring a sacrifice to the Temple and the priest would perform a well-defined ritual that ended with the remains of the sacrifice being burned on the Temple altar.

Here's the point I want to impress upon you. All the sacrifices and the countless animals that died did not forgive one tiny sin. Not one! "Every priest goes to work at the altar each day, offers the same old sacrifices year in, year out, and never makes a dent in the sin problem." (Hebrews 10:11, MSG) At the end of the day no one was forgiven. That seems like a big waste of time and lives with no benefit for which it was intended. However, God had a plan, and the goal was to impress on men the futility of trying to erase sin by religious rituals. None of them work. Not one!

There is only one action that addresses sin and man's standing before God that actually accomplished anything. The sacrifice of Jesus on the cross and the shedding of His blood! He dealt with sin and its consequences when nothing else worked. No remorse, sorrow, confession, repentance or sacrifice done by man can do what Jesus did. His was the only sacrifice that forgave sin and its penalty. "Christ made a single sacrifice for sins, and that was it! Then he sat down right beside God" (Hebrews 10:12b-13, MSG) The sacrifice we must make is to place our unbelief on the Temple altar, and ask Christ to come into our lives. Jesus' one sacrifice dealt with sin. He only asks us to believe in what He did. That's a sacrifice worth doing.

Saints

Every year we celebrate St. Patrick's Day. We also have St. Valentine's Day. When you think about it we have saints everywhere. St. Nicholas at Christmas. All Saints Day. The New Orleans Saints. We have streets named after saints like St. Charles (Who is he?) Rivers like the St. Laurence. Islands like St. Croix and St. Martin. We even have a St. Angelo.

In our politically correct world we should probably change all these saint identifications to meet all the special interest groups. Atheists would change names from St. Patrick to Patrick's Day or No-St. Patrick's Day. Muslims would rename everything with a Mohammad prefix such as Mohammad's Valentine Day. The Federal Government would rename St. Patrick to No-St.-Mohammad-Dude-Dudette-Patrick's Day.

The word saint is derived from the bible and by definition is "most holy thing." I'm not sure the way we use the word today is correct, such as the New Orleans Saints being a "most holy thing," even if they did win the Super Bowl. The scriptures used saints when describing people who had a firm belief in God, and had in one way or another spent their lives serving God. What would make you holy? If you were holy you would automatically be a saint.

Holiness is a word that seems reserved for God. Everyone who studies the bible would agree that God is holy and men are sinners. Hmmm. How do we change sinners into holy saints? The scriptures have the answer to this question, "Yet, now he has reconciled you to himself through the death of Christ in his physical body. As a result, he has brought you into his own presence, and **<u>you are holy and blameless</u>** as you stand before him without a single fault." (Colossians 1:22-23, NLT; emphasis mine) You are made holy because of your relationship to Christ. He is the source of all holiness. If you want to be a saint you have to be reconciled to Him by faith. I guess I could be Saint St. Angelo because of what He did for me. How about you? Are you a saint or still a sinner without Christ?

Salvation and Perfection

"Nobody's perfect!" How many times have you heard that statement? Better still, how many times have you said that about yourself? This is not normally said as a sign of humility declaring that your halo is a bit tilted but still in place. Most often you say it when you've failed at some task or relationship and you're making an excuse for why you didn't measure up. Who could argue with that? We're all human and we all fail at times. Of course, others fail more than we do. Right?

I believe these words were uttered under their breath when Adam and Eve took the plunge into sin by eating of the tree of the knowledge of good and evil. God in His wisdom didn't buy that excuse then and He ain't buying it today. Can you imagine yourself standing before God with all the failures/sins of your life, listed in your autobiography, being held in His hand? God would say to you in that deep voice that resonates around the Universe, "Only perfect people are allowed into My presence and your life has been far from perfect." And you say, "Nobody's perfect!" God would reply, "Do you know how many times I've heard that?" The next sounds you would hear are your knees banging together and your teeth chattering knowing you are in deep trouble. And deep isn't the half of it!

Thank God, there is a better way to meet God. God has a way to make everyone perfect before they ever die and have a face-to-face meeting with Him. "God had planned something better for us so that only together with us would they be made perfect." (Hebrews 11:40, NIV) The plan is to gather all the people who ever lived and make them perfect through His only son Jesus. "Therefore, my friends, I want you to know that through Jesus the forgiveness of sins is proclaimed to you. Through him everyone who believes is set free from every sin, a justification **you were not able to obtain under the law of Moses**." (Acts 13:38-39, NIV; emphasis mine) There it is in black and white. Whoever places their faith in Jesus, by believing He is the Savior, will be made perfect. That way when you meet God the only thing you will hear Him say is, "Well done my good and faithful servant."

Actually there is more to life and death than just being found perfect in God's sight when you meet Him in person. You are perfect right now if you have been born again through faith in Jesus. You are forgiven from all sin and been made the righteousness of God in Christ. I know you are thinking you're just human and "Nobody's perfect," but that is the way "you" see things. Father sees you differently because He sees the glorious work Jesus has done in you. Your perfection in Christ is not just for heaven but it is for here on earth. Start believing like a Believer with a new heart. Start thinking like a Believer with a new mind. Start acting like a Believer with a new family. And start receiving from God like a Believer who is an heir to the Kingdom.

Salvation From Sin

I just saw a curious photograph of the 103rd floor of an office building in Chicago. What made the picture so unusual was a clear glass balcony attached to the otherwise smooth faced surface of the building. The balcony was jutting out about three feet into space and had a glass floor. The intent was to have someone stand in the glass bubble and look bravely down some 103 stories to the busy street below. Just the thought of doing it gives me butterflies. What if the bottom gave way with me standing there? Yikes! A 103-story plunge to the street below. Splat!

We live in a dangerous world. I'm not referring to tall buildings with glass balconies, but the dangers we face just walking around on flat ground. You might be strolling along minding your own business when a slab of glass followed by a 200 pound sightseer hits you on the head. You would be just as flat as if you fell. What if someone grabbed you by the arm and pulled you out of the way of the falling tourist? The person who pulled you to safety would have saved your life.

The bible uses an interesting word to describe such a rescue. It's "saved." The literal translation of the word "saved" from the Greek language, in which the New Testament was written, is "rescued from a dangerous place." That's exactly what Jesus did when He gave His life to save yours. He pulled you out of a dangerous place and into a place of eternal safety. The danger you were in was not falling from a tall building but a mountain of human sin piled over 103 stories high created since the fall of Adam in the Garden of Eden. Every man and woman born on earth since Adam has added to the pile of sin and climbed to it's top.

When you realize you are at the top of a dangerous place and call out to Jesus for help, He gently lifts you from the pile and tenderly places you on level ground in the Kingdom of God. He dresses you in a clean royal robe of righteousness. He places a crown of glory on your head. He inscribes your name in the Lamb's Book of Life. And He promises to be with you always and guide your life away from the treacherous and dangerous mountain of sin. Trusting in Jesus guarantees your safety and keeps you from falling into sin again. "(Jesus) who gave himself for our sins to rescue us from the present evil age..." (Galatians 1:4, NIV)

Shaking the Kingdom

"Don't forget to celebrate Presidents Day on February 20th." And you say, "Who cares?" Probably no one cares but the Presidents. But there is a day worth remembering in February. It's the 14th - Valentine's Day. The day love is in the air and the candy people and restaurants make a fortune. Any man who has any sense will remember his sweetheart on Valentine's Day. Otherwise he might be sleeping in the doghouse on Presidents Day.

Actually, February has been a month that gets very little respect. They keep changing the number of days in the month from 28 to 29 in some feeble attempt to get the calendar in sync with the sun. I don't think its working. The sun seems to be in the same place it's always been. To be honest, I like things that never change so I know where they are when I want to find them. The bible is like that. All the books of the bible are always where they have been for a very long time. New translations pop up every decade or so and a few minor changes get in, but by in large the bible is stable. Do you know what else never changes? The Kingdom of God!

The one thing you can depend on, and place your complete trust in, is God's Kingdom. (Hebrews 12:28, NIV) "Therefore, since we are receiving a kingdom that cannot be shaken, let us be thankful, and so worship God acceptably with reverence and awe." There you have it, the Kingdom can't and won't ever be shaken. Why is that so important? Because every promise of God made in the Kingdom will always be true and no one can change them. God loves you and that will never change. You can bet your life on it. In fact, you can bet your soul on it.

Sheep and Pastors

What makes the best preachers? Nice hair? Inspiring messages? Postgraduate degrees? Some of the best known preachers who had a resume that made them the envy of others, ended up on the junk heap of church history. Perhaps there's some other ingredient that sets a preacher out from the crowd? Since the bible refers to the children of God as sheep, I think a good preacher ought to like sheep. There was a movie back in 1958, starring Glen Ford, titled, "The Sheepman." All through the movie you were led to believe he loved sheep. But at the end you discovered he really loved cows, and had sheep only because he won them in a poker game. I think a lot of preachers are like that; they just put up with the sheep, but don't like them.

Jesus said pastors needed to love and care for the sheep entrusted to them. This sounds easy to do, but lots of men and women get into the ministry because they have false illusions about sheep. Then, after they get close to the sheep, and discover that sheep take a lot of work to care for, they leave the sheep behind and go looking for a better flock.

A good shepherd follows the pattern laid out in Psalms 23. He makes sure the sheep are well cared for with good nourishment from the scriptures. He leads the sheep and doesn't drive them to the place where they can have their spiritual thirst quenched. He cares for their bodily needs and spiritual needs. He makes sure the sheep are led down the right paths of life. He calms their fears when dark shadows fall on their lives. He defends them against all aggressors with his staff. He anoints them with healing oil. He makes sure that the lifestyle of the flock is filled with goodness and mercy. He cares for them and teaches them so that they will always be in God's house on earth, and in His Throne room for all eternity.

There you have it. The only requirement to be a great preacher is to fall in love with the Great Shepherd and His sheep.

Sin and Jelly Bellies

My daughter just presented my granddaughter and me with a Jelly Belly machine. You put in a coin, twist the knob and the Jelly Belly candy begins to fall into the tray. The Jelly Belly candy is a delight to see with all the rainbow of colors and the promise of a sweet taste to the palate. Yum! But you know what? Too much sugar candy is not good for you. Little by little those succulent morsels will decay your teeth, add size to your waist and poison your blood stream. Yuck!

If you can imagine it, you are an empty Jelly Belly machine when you are born. Then the devil fills you with all varieties of sinful ideas. You start enjoying his temptations and before you know it you are filled to the brim with sin and that sin has a high cost associated with it. You try getting rid of sins one at a time as if you were putting coins into the Jelly Belly machine. But it never gets empty because you keep adding candy (sin) to it.

God saw the problem that causes us to fill our lives with sins and He provided a solution. The solution was Jesus, His Only begotten Son. Jesus took all our sins and nailed them to the cross when He died. Every sin we have ever committed or will ever commit was removed from us when He died. "He is the atoning sacrifice for our sins, and not only for ours but also for the sins of the whole world." (1 John 2:2, NIV) Our problem is solved if we believe that and invite Him into our lives.

In closing lets get back to the Jelly Belly machine. I LOVE Jelly Bellies! I don't care that the candy is bad for me. I'm going to eat them with my granddaughter until they are all gone, then I'm going to buy some more. How foolish is that? You know what? That's how some folks are about their sins. They refuse to invite Jesus into their lives and keep eating the candy of life. How foolish is that?

Sorrow and Tragedy

Danny Gokey, an American Idol contestant, recorded a song titled, "My Best Days Are Ahead of Me." This song spoke volumes about Danny because life has not always been good to him. He was doing faithful service for God as a worship leader in his church. He had a new wife. He was making plans to audition for the American Idol show. He was living the dream. Suddenly, four weeks prior to the audition, tragedy pierced his bubble of happiness when he least expected it. His beautiful young wife got sick and died leaving him a widower at an age when their life together was just beginning. How did Danny, and others like him, overcome such calamities?

Happiness needs to be based on something bigger and stronger than the uninvited events that buffet your small ship of life. What is the substance that holds you together when the waves crash over the bow? What plugs up the holes that suddenly materialize and your life raft starts sinking? What will save you when you're going down for the third and final time, gasping for one more breath of air? Danny knew. And so did the songwriter who wrote, "My Best Days Are Ahead of Me." He too had lost his young wife and was later inspired the write that song.

You need an unsinkable ship. You need rarified air. You need the presence of God to lift you when you're tumbling beneath the waves. The bible says you have a friend in Christ who will stick closer than a brother. You need God who lifted Danny and every other believer in troubled waters. This is not a panacea of wishful phony religious rhetoric. This is the truth that will let you sing that old hymn written by a man who lost his wife and children at sea. His song says in part: *When sorrows like sea billows roll; Whatever my lot, Thou has taught me to say, "It is well, it is well, with my soul."* Or Danny's lyrics that say: *Blowing out the candles on another birthday cake. Old enough to look back and laugh at my mistakes. Young enough to look at the future and like what I see. My best days are ahead of me.* Give God a chance; He wants to sing with you again.

Soul Salvation

The most important war as far as you are concerned is the War for Your Soul. You are going to leave this world one day and find yourself in eternity. That day will be the most accelerating emotional day you will ever experience, filled with a kaleidoscope of sensory overload, when you see God in all of His glory. Or, it will be a day of diabolical horror, filled with evil beyond measure. In simple terms you will exit life and find yourself in heaven or hell. There is a battle being waged for your soul this very day. The outcome of that war determines your final destination.

I recently met a woman in her eighties who was on her deathbed. I had been invited to visit with her and to pray for her to be healed. Before I prayed for her I asked her about her relationship to God and she replied that she thought there was a supreme being but that Jesus, heaven, and hell were just concepts made up by men to control societies. I took a few moments and explained to her the story of Jesus from the bible and how He took her sin upon Himself at Calvary and died for her so she could go to heaven. (See Romans 10:9-10) I asked her if she wanted to invite Him into her life with a simple prayer of faith. She politely declined. I asked her if she still wanted me to pray for her healing with the understanding I would pray in the name of Jesus. She agreed and I prayed. Several days later she passed into eternity. But before she died she dictated a brief letter to me that said in part, "I have never had the pleasure of having the concept (of Jesus) so deeply explained. It was as though a deep concentration of meditation was put into me as you read the bible." Her loved ones, who where at her side when she slipped into eternity, said she lifted both her arms toward heaven and gently passed over.

I relate this story about that dear lady because she typifies the war for souls. All her life Satan was winning the war with lies and doubts he placed into her heart and mind. She had never been told the truth that Jesus won the war for her soul when He died and defeated death, hell, and the grave. Her letter assured me that she had accepted Christ into her life. It wasn't a textbook programmed prayer of salvation. It was a simple encounter with Christ that brought eternal life to her soul. I believe as she lifted her arms to Him, He repeated the words to her that He spoke to the thief next to Him on the cross, *"Today, you will be with me in paradise.*" Whatever you do, don't wait any longer to place your trust in Jesus. Ask Him into your life today. Oh, in case you think my healing prayer was not very good since she died, keep in mind that the greatest healing is the healing of the soul.

Tear Down Wall Street

"Tear down Wall Street!" is the cry of some of the people in America today. Wall Street has become, to some, the symbol of what's wrong. It divides between those who "have" and those who "have not." Walls breed contempt and hatred. People stand of either side of walls and hurl everything from words to grenades across the top. Walls can surround cities, divide nations, mark off lines of ownership, and a host of other things we want to protect and claim as ours. Walls are made of stones, barbed wire, electricity, and wood. But the walls that are the most difficult to breach and tear down are the walls of ideas.

The Apostle Paul highlighted a wall of ideas that existed in, of all places, the revered Temple of the Jews in Jerusalem. He called it the "the dividing wall of hostility" in Ephesians 2:14. This wall separated the Jews from the Gentiles. The divide was so severe, and filled with hatred, between these two groups of people, that the "people of God," the Jews, built a physical wall in the Temple court and commanded the Gentiles to keep out. The wall was about four feet high and every so many feet across the length of the wall were warning signs etched in stone that said that no Gentile, on the pain of death, was to pass through that wall.

Churches are great about building walls of hostility. We declare that anyone who doesn't meet our standards of righteousness cannot come on our side of the wall. We name our walls Baptist, Catholic, Methodist, Lutheran etc. We put up warning signs that declare that those on the other side of our walls are in great danger of spiritual death. You must be baptized according to a certain formula. You cannot receive communion with us. You must be converted before you can marry one of us. The list goes on and on ad infinitum.

Jesus had another idea. He said, "Come to me, all you who are weary and burdened, and I will give you rest." (Matthew 11:28, NIV) He claimed to be a door not a wall. He gave invitations to come in, not to be shut out. You might say that we need walls because we're right and others are wrong. Churches and people may have walls to keep others out, but Jesus has doors to let outsiders in. His invitation is for you to come to Him.

Ten Commandments

Have you ever heard any of the following statements? "You better behave yourself! Just wait until your father gets home." "How many times do I need to tell you what to do?" "What were you thinking when you did that?" "Don't ever play with fire!" "Drugs will destroy you." "Just say, 'No!'" I know you have because they are imbedded into the fabric of our society. The big question I have is, do they work? Do they actually change behavior for the better? Judging by what we see and hear these days I suspect they do little if any good.

God had the same idea about modifying the behavior of His best creation – us. "Just give them a list of rules to follow and everything will be okay," God told Moses. The formula to make the list was, "Thou shall not… (blank)," and then fill in the blank. Actually God dictated the list to Moses and we still have it today. The ten Thou Shall Nots. Upon reflection, after God gave these instruction, I think He realized that His plan was not working very well.

Paul, God's number one New Testament writer said it this way, "Nevertheless, I would not have known what sin was had it not been for the law. For I would not have known what coveting really was if the law had not said, 'You shall not covet.'" (Romans 7:7, NIV) He then went on to say that he found in his life that when the law told him not to do something, he somehow did more of it. There seems to be a defective DNA spot in us that just loves to break the law of God. Think about this. Have you ever lied? Coveted? Wanted what someone else owned? Took another person's spouse? You might say I did a few of these things but I didn't murder anyone. Sorry, you don't get a gold ring. The bible says if you break one commandment, you've broken them all. And the penalty for breaking any of them is death.

The Good News is God instituted a plan B. He saw how bad a job we were doing and sent His Son who took the death penalty for our sins when He died on the cross. His single sacrifice made it possible for us to be forgiven and receive eternal life. Now that's really Good News! Don't forget this! It's important.

Thanks to Founding Fathers

I'm so glad our country decided long ago to set aside a day of Thanksgiving for all that God has done for us. President Washington in 1789 made the following proclamation:

"Whereas it is the duty of all Nations to acknowledge the providence of almighty God, to obey his will, to be grateful for his benefits, and humbly to implore his protection and favor - and Whereas both Houses of Congress have by their joint Committee requested me "to recommend to the People of the United States a day of public thanksgiving and prayer to be observed by acknowledging with grateful hearts the many signal favors of Almighty God, "

There you have it! The President and both Houses of Congress acknowledged that there is a God and that we as citizens should thank Him for the many favors the Almighty God has provided. If the President and Congress had waited until 2010 to inaugurate such a tradition of Thanksgiving it might have read something like this: *"Whereas it is the duty of all Nations to guess whether there is an Almighty God. And in the interest of not offending anyone we acknowledge Buddha, Allah, sacred cows, voodoo, sticks, stones, the intelligence of man, the almighty governments around the world and any unknown god we may have missed – and we recommend a day of public thanksgiving and prayer to any and all of the aforementioned gods knowing full well there may not be any gods anywhere, and further declare that none of these thanks can take place in any public school, building or grounds within borders of the United States of America."*

I don't know about you but I choose to stick with our first President George Washington and ignore the pinheads in Washington D.C. I think if President Washington were alive he'd make them take his name off the city of the federal government and just call it D.C. which stands for "Dumb Congress."

Hey, you know what? God is still God, and is still worthy of our thanks. Thank you God for America and for men and women like George Washington across this great nation. Father, You founded it and we still believe in You and we still believe it's "One

Nation Under God." "And whatever you do, whether in word or deed, do it all in the name of the Lord Jesus, giving thanks to God the Father through him." (Colossians 3:17, NIV)

Thanksgiving

When you hear, "Gentlemen start your engines!" at the Indianapolis 500 auto race, you know there's going to be a lot of loud noises caused by a host of people going as fast as they can, for as long as they can in Formula 1 racing machines. When you hear the words, "Happy Thanksgiving!" you know there's going to be a lot of deceased turkeys and most Americans will end up in a near comatose sleep after those sacrificial birds have been ingested. "Burp!" is the most heard sound from sea to shining sea.

Where have we gone wrong? Thanksgiving has been so distorted; we now have created a follow up day and named it "Black Friday." How did giving thanks to God for caring for the first settlers on our shores get turned into a food fest? And how did the food fest get followed by a shop-till-you-drop spending frenzy? Hey, I'm not opposed to family time around a table full of food, nor am I opposed to stirring the economy with faux-sales the day after. I just think somebody needs to say, "Thanksgiving" was designated as a day to say "Thank You" to God for all the blessings He has given to the people of America.

Done at the City of Washington, this Third day of October, in the year of our Lord one thousand eight hundred and sixty-three... Abraham Lincoln proclaimed an annual day of Thanksgiving. The proclamation reads in part.

> *It has seemed to me fit and proper that they should be solemnly, reverently and gratefully acknowledged as with one heart and one voice by the whole American People. I do therefore invite my fellow citizens in every part of the United States, and also those who are at sea and those who are sojourning in foreign lands, to set apart and observe the last Thursday of November next, as a day of Thanksgiving and Praise to our beneficent Father who dwelleth in the Heavens.* (Source: *Collected Works of Abraham Lincoln*, edited by Roy P. Basler.)

How about this Thanksgiving we follow the admonition of our great president Abraham Lincoln, and have a day of "Thanksgiving and Praise." Who knows? We might revive a great old American tradition. One last item - I wonder when we dropped the "Praise" from the "Thanksgiving and Praise" Mr. Lincoln proclaimed? Must have been the work of the ACLU. (Sorry, I couldn't help myself.) Have a wonderful Thanksgiving and don't forget the "Praise."

The End of a Terrorist

The Munchkins, in the Wizard of Oz, sang "Ding-dong the witch is dead. Which old witch? The wicked witch!" when they witnessed the end of their arch nemesis, the Wicked Witch of the East. Most of the free world felt like the Oz's Munchkins at the news that Osama Bin Laden had been taken out by a host of Navy SEALS.

I found that I had mixed emotions. Part of me was elated that someone as evil as Bin Laden was no longer breathing and could not inflict any more pain and suffering on mankind. Yet, another part of me questioned whether, as a believing Christian, I should be celebrating the death of a human being. As a leader in the Christian community, was I giving a Christ-like response to the demise of this evil man by being happy he was dead?

There were several thoughts that ran through my mind. I knew the people who had lost loved ones on

9/11 would be relieved and experience some kind of closure. I understood the joy of those people outside the White House who were waving flags and shouting "USA! USA!" at the news of Bin Laden's death. I felt that the military across the globe, from West Point to the foxholes in Afghanistan, were experiencing the pride of a job well done. But what about me?

I pondered what the source of my moral bearings, the Bible, said about this. It says, "Thou shall not kill." The best Bible scholars all agree this mean we cannot murder anyone. Self-defense, for example, is ample justification to kill someone. Heaven knows that, on more than one occasion, God instructed His people to kill everything in sight when they went to war. King David, "a man after God's heart" had killed so many people we have no record of the actual count. Revelation, the last book in the bible, tells of a final battle where the bloodshed would be as high as the bridle of a horse.

I found my answer in the authority given to governments by God. God entrusts governments with the welfare of its citizens. Two scriptures set the principles of government's authority. "Everyone must submit himself to the governing authorities, for there is no authority except that which God has established.

The authorities that exist have been established by God... For rulers hold no terror for those who do right, but for those who do wrong... (Romans 13:1, 3a, NIV) So we are to submit to governing authorities and they have the right to inflict "terror" on those who do wrong. This of course does not give them authority to ask us to participate in evil as Hitler did in Nazi Germany.

I believe the government had the right to pursue and punish Bin Laden. I am happy and will sleep better knowing he has been brought to justice for his crimes. But, I can't sing along with the Munchkins, even if the personification of Oz's evil witch has died. I take no jubilation in anyone, even Bin Laden, meeting God before they meet Jesus Christ as their Savior.

The Way to Walk

I had the privilege of meeting a man and his wife last week who had spent several years of their lives living and ministering in Turkey. Now normally the only turkey I'm interested in, is the one who comes to dinner for Thanksgiving. Yum. But back to my story. The nation of Turkey is home to the ancient city of Ephesus of biblical fame. Since I was right in the middle of a sermon series on the book of Ephesians, I was overjoyed to meet someone who had actually been there. Between forks of food I asked as many questions as I could. Seeing Ephesus through their eyes was very enlightening.

One of the most interesting aspects of Ephesus is that its marble streets were engraved with road signs. Not the kind we see today that tell us to "stop" or "yield," but signs chiseled into the marble roadways to give direction to travelers. They carved the shape of a foot pointing in a certain direction and etched a picture of where the foot was pointing. "The Temple is this way!" or "The library is this way!" The thought that excited me was that over 7 times (depending on the translation you use) Paul wrote the words "walk" or "way" as he instructed the Ephesian people. He took something everyone in the ancient city knew, and used it as a signpost to direct them to something new.

Paul's signs said, "Walk this way in the Kingdom of God" or "Walk this way to a life of faith." or "Walk this way in love." or "Walk this way in your relationships." The streets of ancient Ephesus didn't lead to the God of Paul. They led instead to temples of false gods, places were immorality was practiced, and places that lead to misery and death. "All of us also lived among them at one time, gratifying the cravings of our flesh and following its desires and thoughts. Like the rest, we were by nature deserving of wrath." (Ephesians 2:3, NIV) Yes, the people of Ephesus lived in a city that was prosperous and beautiful beyond imagination, but it was a pathway to eternal destruction.

Jesus said of Himself, "I am The Way". The early church was referred to as "The Way." The Way to what? The way that leads to God! Listen to the words of Jesus about the way in which we walk.

"Enter through the narrow gate; for the gate is wide and the way is broad that leads to destruction, and there are many who enter through it. For the gate is small and the way is narrow that leads to life, and there are few who find it." (Matthew 7:13-14, NAS) Which way are you walking? Try walking in the footsteps of Jesus, Paul, and a host of other followers of "The Way" that leads to life. Walk this Way!

There Is Hope For You

There is a Golden Labrador Retriever named Buddy in my neighborhood. Buddy is the coolest dog in town. He is never in a bad mood. Never barks. Never bites. Never chases cars. Buddy loves to slink down his driveway and lay stretched out on his side and while away the hours in the warmth of the sun. He only moves when his master drives up. He either moves or gets run over. Buddy is the perfect dog. However, Buddy has a dark side.

That dark side of Buddy is that he is a thief. Yes, it's hard to believe such a great dog would steal but he does. He is like an experienced jewel thief who knows exactly what he wants and when no one is watching he creeps through the neighborhood, looking around to make sure no one sees him, and then he goes into action. What is his specialty? Newspapers!

If you don't get up before Buddy you will never get to read a newspaper without Buddy's teeth marks in it. He doesn't mean to be the neighborhood paper crook but he seems unable to restrain himself. You see Buddy is a lot like most of us. We don't mean to do things we shouldn't do, but we find ourselves slinking around and doing what we're ashamed of all the time. Most of the time we are cool people, but then there's that dark side.

Paul, the great apostle who wrote most of the New Testament, had a dark side too. He said in his letter to the Romans: "I realize that I don't have what it takes. I can will it, but I can't do it. I decide to do good, but I don't really do it; I decide not to do bad, but then I do it anyway. My decisions, such as they are, don't result in actions. Something has gone wrong deep within me and gets the better of me every time." (Romans 7:18-20, MSG) Yes, Paul had a Buddy problem. The fact is we all have a Buddy problem. So what are we to do?

The bad behavior problem that we all have can't be resolved with will power alone. We need a power outside of ourselves to enable us to deal with our behavior. Paul tells us; "I've tried everything and nothing helps. I'm at the end of my rope. Is there no one who can do anything for me? Isn't that the real question? The answer, thank God, is that Jesus Christ can and does." (Romans 7:24-25a, MSG)

The answer to all of life's bad habitual problems is Jesus. He can help you if you just ask Him to. Paul did. Millions of others after Paul did. And you can too. "But what about Buddy?" you might ask. I don't know. Pray for him. Who knows what God might do?

Thoughts

Does it really matter what you think?

"What in the world were they thinking?" is a rhetorical question we have asked over and over as society has shifted from right to left. The logic that is used is so illogical it would make Mr. Spock's ears wilt. Actually, society in America has shifted from Christian values to deist/atheist values. Not right to left. So what is going on? The answer is there is a war raging and it's a war for thoughts.

Rick Warren said, "When we change the way people think, we change the way they believe and ultimately the way they act." So the battle for the way people act begins in the way they think about life and the solutions to life. One of the most contested thoughts today is what you think about abortion. At one time when a woman was pregnant it was thought that she had a baby in her womb. Since it was a baby, that unborn child had value, and the mother and all of society did everything it could to preserve and protect that life. Then a significant change happened. The unborn child was renamed a fetus. As such it had no real value since it was classified as excess tissue growing in the womb and could be destroyed with no consequences. So society began to think the child was a piece of tissue and could be aborted. The way society acted changed because it changed the way it thought. We don't have an exact count but it is estimated that over 50 million babies have be murdered because society thinks differently about pregnant moms.

It matters what you think about things. The enemies of Christ are always trying to change the way you think and get you over to their side. Those who are aligned with the Judeo-Christian values of America need to wage war against those intent on changing our way of thinking and our lives. The scriptures say, "We demolish arguments and every pretension that sets itself up against the knowledge of God, and we take captive every <u>thought</u> to make it obedient to Christ." (2 Corinthians 10:5, NIV) There is a war for thoughts and what you think about that war will determine your actions in the war.

True Love

Valentine's Day is a special holiday when we proclaim love for someone special. Have you noticed that it is politically correct to love others? There is no hue and cry by the "hate others" group to have an equal day throughout the world. Interesting thought isn't it? I think it's safe to say everyone wants to love and be loved. It's universal. But how do you know when you love someone or they love you?

Most love relationships flourish when love is returned in kind. In other words, we love as long as we're loved. Is that true Valentine Day love? The scriptures have a lot to say about love. God loves us. Love each other. Jesus loves you. In fact, one scripture that is read at more weddings than any other is the definition of love that ends, "Love never gives up, never loses faith, is always hopeful, and endures through every circumstance." (1 Corinthians 13:7, NLT) Wow! Love "never" gives up or loses faith. It's "always" hopeful. That's a far cry from what I see as I counsel couples whose love has dimmed and been replaced with hurt and bitterness.

The truth is that love, as we use that word, has lots to do with the way we feel and very little with the way we act toward each other. True love as defined in the scriptures is, "Love is patient and kind. Love is not jealous or boastful or proud or rude. It does not demand its own way. It is not irritable, and it keeps no record of being wronged. It does not rejoice about injustice but rejoices whenever the truth wins out." (1 Corinthians 13:4-6, NLT) Think about it. Love is something we "do," not something we feel. We can choose to be kind and patient. We can choose to not be jealous. In fact, every element of love is something we can choose to do or not do. So the next time you tell someone you love him or her, ask yourself this question: "Do my actions demonstrate my words?" .

Trust God

The naysayers of America say, "We are tired of the Christian Right-Wing Radicals telling us what to do. It's time to get you, and all your ancient rhetoric, out of America. We have had enough of you!" Or in the words of the Reverend Jeremiah Wright (Wrong), "God d_ _ m, America!"

The truth is that the only glue holding the United States of America together is the glue on the bindings on the Christian Bibles. If God and His people leave, which they will one day in the rapture, America will cease to exist. Oh, there might be a nation using the name, but the United States that was birthed in 1776 with a faith in God, will be relegated to fading history.

Many are the days when God's people scratch their heads and wonder if God will ever show up to straighten the mess they see every day. "Under God" was omitted from the Pledge of Allegiance by that bastion of truth, NBC, and its sibling, MSNBC. What about the VFW volunteers who honor veterans by officiating at their funerals that have been instructed not to use God or Jesus' name? *VA (Veterans Affairs) Forbids Mention of God at Funerals for Veterans and Requires Families to Submit Prayer for Approval to the Government.* (Veterans Resources, June 29, 2011) God where are you?????

Job, that model of unwarranted suffering, had a conversation with God in the last few chapters of the Bible-book that carries his name. The dialogue began when Job asked God why he had suffered so much. After all, he had done nothing wrong. God's reply was not so much an answer, as it was showing Job the bigger picture.

God asked Job what he had done to create and care for the world. God said, "Who is this that questions my wisdom with such ignorant words?" (Job 38:2, NLT) To which Job replied, "You asked, 'Who is this that questions my wisdom with such ignorance?' It is I—and I was talking about things I knew nothing about, things far too wonderful for me." (Job 42:3, NLT) Job's answer to God was an obvious, "Nothing."

You may not like what's going on, and I hope you don't, but God has not looked away at the injustice and blasphemy that is happening. He has a bigger plan and its up to His people to trust Him. In the words of that singing philosopher, Elvis Presley, God is T.C.B. (Taking Care of Business). Read the last chapter of Job and you will see what I mean.

Unshakable Kingdom

I woke up the day after the last national election to discover that the sun was still in the sky and the earth was still spinning on its axis. (Although it is tilted a bit more to the left.) I've lived long enough to learn that change comes whether you want it to or not. Your kids grow up. Your finances change. Your weight changes. Governments change. This process has a four letter word to describe it. It's called LIFE! How you cope with the changes of life determines the quality of YOUR life. My dad, the great life-psychologist, who had a 4th grade education, put it this way, "Son, life goes on."

So how do you cope with the winds of life? You hang onto something that cannot change. Now, I realize I just said everything changes, and now I'm suggesting you hang onto something that never changes. What never changes is God! The Word of God never changes. The sacrifice of Jesus for your sins never changes. Yesterday never changes. Your spouse never changes. (I just said that to lighten you up.) The truth, according to the bible, is that everything changes except the things that really matter. And the things that really matter, in the long run, are the eternal truths. God cannot be defeated. The Kingdom of God cannot be shaken. And believers in Jesus Christ can experience stability in the midst of an ever-changing world.

God said that every created thing would be shaken. The earth, the heavens, and your life will continue to be shaken. But He also said that those who believe and trust in Him would receive a gift that could never be shaken. "Therefore, since we are receiving a kingdom that cannot be shaken, let us be thankful, and so worship God acceptably with reverence and awe." (Hebrews 12:28, NIV) We can survive and be victorious in life if we will just hang onto God and His eternal kingdom. Jesus said it this way, "Be of good cheer. I have overcome the world." Take a look inside your bible and read Philippians chapter 4. You will see that all the promises of God are still there. Yahoo!!!

Valentine's Day

Valentine's Day is a big day in the life of most Americans. The origin of the day as a time for romance is very murky. It could be as old as the Roman Empire or as new as the 1700-1800 era. Even more mysterious is St. Valentine. No one can prove such a man ever existed. But of this we can be certain, St. Valentine, like Santa Clause, is here to stay. Every woman, every jewelry store, every restaurant and every Hallmark Card will keep this romantic tradition going and growing forever.

At the very center of the mystique of Valentine's Day is love. This four letter word has been the driving force behind boy girl relationships since Adam first stammered to Eve, "I... I...love you." It worked for him and every other romance since then.

Love is prevalent in the scriptures, but not just romantic love, such as seen in the Old Testament book, "The Song of Solomon," but in virtually every relationship. We are commanded to love God. This is followed up with an admonition to love our neighbors. However, more importantly than us loving God is the fact He loves us. He loves us so much that He sent His only begotten Son to die for us. Now that's love! It's interesting that the pathway to heaven is not that we love God but that we believe that He loves us. Our love for Him is a response to His love for us. "We love because he first loved us." (1 John 4:19, NIV) Jesus goes on to say that people would know that we love God by the way we love each other. "By this everyone will know that you are my disciples, if you love one another." (John 13:35, NIV)

So, lets not give St. Valentine a bad rap because we can't verify his pedigree. He has stirred us to demonstrate our love by the way we treat the ones we love. By the way guys, flowers shout really loud, "I love you" sometimes better than the words themselves. Have a great St. Valentine's Day!

Validation

Isn't it amazing how easily we can become legends in our own minds? Where do you go to get validation for your identity? Is it words of praise from others? Your job? Your possessions? Your education? Your finances? Your spouse? Your children? What makes the endorphins in your body fire-off and give you that sense of well-being and acceptance in life? Do you need to be confirmed by someone or something to make you feel good? Interesting thoughts, don't you think?

All of us have a natural tendency to depend on outside influences to make us feel good about ourselves. This is not necessarily bad, but if that's all that makes us want to get up in the morning, we will discover that we will always need another fix to get high. We will depend on our personal version of drugs to induce artificial highs.

There is a stimulus available for our lives that will never run dry. Jesus met a woman one day at a drinking well who was addicted to external pleasures. She always needed something new to make her day. She thirsted for things that would never satisfy her parched soul. Her dependence on things led her to marry and divorce five times and when Jesus found her, she was living with a man who was not her husband. Jesus said to her that if she knew who He was, and asked Him for a drink of "living water," it would satisfy all her needs for all eternity. "Everyone who drinks this (worldly) water will be thirsty again, but whoever drinks the water I give him will never thirst. Indeed, the water I give him will become in him a spring of water welling up to eternal life." (John 4:13–14, NIV)

You see our true identity in life stems from our relationship to God. It's letting Him validate us. He alone can give us a well of joy that is not dependent on this world's perishing trinkets and accolades, but on His voice that call us to be His sons and daughters. It's His words that direct our lives. It's His presence that fills our every need. It's His stamp of approval that proclaims to your heart, "Well done my good and faithful servant."

Waiting on God

I hate to wait for anything! I started hating to wait when I was young and it has been with me all of my life. Waiting for Christmas. Waiting for my birthday. Waiting for my grades in school. Waiting in line. Yikes! Just the thought of waiting gives me a headache. I guess what I don't like about waiting is that whatever I'm waiting for is out of my control. And I love being in control.

When I became a Christian, I quickly learned that Christians spend a good portion of their lives waiting. I halfway thought that being a Believer and a member of the Kingdom of God would eliminate my need to wait for anything. I thought I'd pray and instantly my prayers would be answered. Not! I soon experienced that you pray and then wait. Wait? That's the last thing I want to do. It's that old control issue again. I want to steer my ship of life.

Soon after I entered the Kingdom, God began to speak to me about serving Him and my need to attend seminary. I hate school more than I hate waiting. But God opened the opportunity for me to attend seminary and I arrived with great expectations of entering the ministry upon completion of my studies.

Two years later, when I finished my tour in school, the old wait issue reappeared. I expected the First Church of Somewhere to call and invite me to be their pastor. I actually sat by the phone and waited for it to ring. One week became a month and a month turned into half a year. No calls... not a chirp. My enthusiasm began to fade and my hopes were being crushed. What had I done wrong? Where was God? What do I do now? My wife Pat, in her wisdom, asked me what was the last word I was sure that I had heard from God. I searched my memory and told her He said, "Wait on the Lord." Pat asked, "Why don't you just enjoy the wait?" Wow! Words of wisdom from the heart of God spoken to me via my wife.

That day I decided to do whatever I could to serve God. I volunteered for any job I could get at my home church and started to enjoy my journey. Here I am about 35 years later still enjoying the wait. You see my expectation of ministry was not God's plan for me. He is in control of my life. "But if we look forward to something we don't yet have, we must wait patiently and confidently." (Romans 8:25, NLT)

Waiting, as I've finally learned, is not so bad when you're waiting on God. If you're waiting on God for an answer, kick back, relax, and enjoy the wait.

War on 9/11

I was at church quietly praying about the current circumstances of my life. God bless my children. God bless my wife. God bless my church. Etc. To my irritation, my cell phone began to chirp. I looked at it to see who was interrupting my prayer time. I saw it was my wife so I answered. She told me a plane had just crashed into the World Trade Center in New York. Pat's voice gave me a slight sense of urgency. I hung up the phone. Then hung up on God. Shortly, I arrived home, sat before the TV and watched the smoke rising from the WTC tower. With no warning the second tower burst into flame. My mind raced to make sense of what my eyes were taking in. Two planes in one day? What? Huh? …… Then realization set in. This was no accident!

We soon learned that a third plane had decimated the Pentagon. A fourth crashed in Pennsylvania. The President soon announced we were at war. New words became part of our vocabulary: Al-Qaeda. Osama Ben Laden. Jihad. A new panorama of sights, sounds, places and people rose to a level of importance in our lives.

This world we reside in is filled with unexpected events that shatter our peace. Some are personal, like sickness or losing a love one. Others have worldwide reverberations like 9/11. What can the common man do to keep himself steady as the world beneath his feet shudders? There is a scripture that can give us help. "All of creation will be shaken and removed, so that only unshakable things will remain. Since we are receiving a Kingdom that is unshakable, let us be thankful and please God by worshiping him with holy fear and awe." (Hebrews 12:27-28, NLT) The Kingdom of God cannot be shaken. We would be wise to put our faith and trust in God, so that when the world trembles, we can have His peace that will keep us steady in a trembling world.

Weak Made Strong

Why are you strong when you feel weak?

Sometimes on Sunday mornings as I sit in my office going over the sermon I've prepared to preach that day, I wonder if I ought to just run away and hide until after the services are over. My notes look like something a fifth grader put together instead of a seasoned minister of the gospel. But instead of jumping off the springboard of doubt and despair into the pool of desperation, I pack my briefcase and head toward the church building whispering the inadequate prayer, "Help me Lord..."

Then when the worship music stops and I step up to the podium, something wonderful happens. My notes are clear, my voice is strong, my spirit is strengthened and the Word of the Lord is spoken to the hearts of the congregation. After the service I will be approached by members of the congregation who say things like, "Thank you pastor, what you said was just what I needed today." I smile and utter a gracious "Thank you," knowing God deserves the thanks not me.

It's all about Him! He is the anointing! He is the power! He is the wisdom of the ages! Believers are just vessels in His hands. Without Him we are nothing and with Him we are voices that can change the world. "Now you have every spiritual gift you need as you eagerly wait for the return of our Lord Jesus Christ." (1 Corinthians 1:7, NLT) In Christ, we have "every spiritual gift you need." He understands that in our weakness we gain His strength. The gifts that he has empowered mortal men with flow in abundance to accomplish His will when we depend only on Him.

So the next time you feel ill equipped to do what God has chosen you to do, remember you have every spiritual gift, and it may seem foolish to you at times, but it is the power of God at work in you.

Weapons of Warfare

There was a great line from the movie, "The Untouchables," when Sean Connery pulled a gun on a mafia hit man who was holding a knife. "You brought a knife to a gunfight?" Connery exclaimed. Have you ever been poorly equipped to handle a confrontation you've been involved in? Someone outwits you in business. Your children are in trouble and you don't know what to do. Your spouse and you fight more than George Forman. You're in financial trouble again. The list goes on and on.

Maybe you're bringing a knife to a gunfight. The bible tells us "For though we live in the world, we do not wage war as the world does. The weapons we fight with are not the weapons of the world." (2 Corinthians 10:3-5, NIV) So we do not wage war like the world and our weapons are not of the world. God is saying that when we fight and use worldly tactics, we are doomed to failure. There are spiritual forces at work against you and those forces cannot to defeated with worldly warfare. "For our struggle is not against flesh and blood, but against the rulers, against the authorities, against the powers of this dark world and against the spiritual forces of evil in the heavenly realms." (Ephesians 6:12, NIV)

The forces against you have an agenda. They want you defeated, depressed and hopeless. They want you to throw up your hands in surrender. However, to the contrary, God wants you to live in victory. He wants you to prosper in your finances. He wants you to live in health. He wants your children following Him. He wants your marriage to be in harmony. You live defeated because you're thinking like the world instead of like Christ. Jesus is the answer to all of life's problems. When men are addicted – We offer Christ. When marriages are in trouble – We offer Christ. When sickness rages – We offer Christ. When hope is all gone – We offer Christ. Christ is not a weapon against evil; He is "the victory" over evil. Put your puny dull pocketknives away and pick up The Sword of the Lord – The Word of God. Then you will see victory in every area of your life.

What Does The Future Hold?

I used to travel frequently by air in my business. I was always nervous when we took off in horrible weather and the plane was being pushed in every direction as we bounced into the sky. The blackness, storms of rain or snow, always kept my prayer life at its best. "Please Lord keep us safe!" was my silent plea. Then as the plane gained speed and altitude we would enter the dark zone of clouds that made the wings disappear. "Pleaseeeeeee….." I continued my near panic prayers. Then, with no warning, the plane would burst out of the darkness into the sparkling blue of a magnificent light filled sky. The plane would settle down and my white knuckles would gain color as I let go of the arms of the seat. "Thanks, Lord." I would sigh as we made our way at 30,000 feet to our destination.

Living is a lot like flying with lots of unknowns, bouncing, darkness, breathtaking views, and countless highs and lows. We find ourselves shouting,

"Wheeeeee" in the highs and pleading, "Pleaseeeeee" in the lows, as we go from experience to experience. We are about to wave goodbye to the present year and enter a new and exciting year filled with possibilities. Many of us have experienced the worst year of our lives. Others wish the present year would never end. But no matter how this year was, the new year is rushing towards us.

One thing I was certain of when I used to fly – what goes up will come down. That's an unchangeable fact of flying around this celestial globe. You can bet your life on it. There's something else you can bet your life on. God is the pilot who controls the events of the future and nothing will happen without His knowledge. I'm not sure what the new year will hold for us, but I know God can carry you through the worst weather it has to offer. Look at what the bible says about your life. "Therefore I tell you, do not worry about your life, what you will eat or drink; or about your body, what you will wear. Is not life more than food, and the body more than clothes? Look at the birds of the air; they do not sow or reap or store away in barns, and yet your heavenly Father feeds them. Are you not much more valuable than they? Can any one of you by worrying add a single hour to your life? (Matthew 6:25-27, NIV) But seek first his kingdom and his righteousness, and all these things will be given to you as well." (Matthew 6:33 NIV) How about trusting your pilot, Jesus, to fly you through the future and trust Him to find a way to bring you safely home?

What If Heaven Were Closed Today?

What if heaven were closed for a day due to unexpected repairs to the Pearly Gates? No one could enter Heaven, so no Christians could die that day. Obviously, this would have no effect on those destined for hell. (Sorry.) And, while the repair crew was working on the Pearly Gates, they accidentally knocked out the prayer line so no one's prayers were able to get through to Prayer Central. The treasures that believers normally send up to Heaven for storage until they died would pile up outside the Gates. What a mess!

Thank God this can never happen, at least as far as I know. So we can pray and send up our treasures and if you're ready you can die and go to heaven today if you want to. (No takers?) I know this is kind of silly but how is your prayer life? Would it make any difference to you if Heaven was open or closed as far as your prayers are concerned? Are you sending daily prayers to Heaven? God expects us to be praying every day all day long. "Rejoice always, **pray continually**, give thanks in all circumstances; for this is God's will for you in Christ Jesus." (1 Thessalonians 5:16-18, NIV; emphasis mine) How do you measure your communication to heaven when compared to this scripture? Do you rejoice always? Do you pray continually? Do you give thanks in all circumstances? I think it's interesting that for most of us we would not know if Heaven were closed for repairs based on our communications there.

What about our treasures in transit? We send so few treasures to Heaven that when we get there our mansions will be thread-bear and empty. "Don't hoard treasure down here where it gets eaten by moths and corroded by rust or—worse!—stolen by burglars. **Stockpile treasure in heaven**, where it's safe from moth and rust and burglars." (Matthew 6:19-20, MSG; emphasis mine)

So, do you know if Heaven is open today based on your prayers and treasures sent there? Give it a test and send up a prayer or a treasure right now and see if it's open. You will know immediately if it's closed for repairs.

When You Fall

"Help! I've fallen and I can't get up," has crept into our clichés, thanks to First Alert. I feel I need an emergency button to push sometimes. The cares and pressures of life have a way of tripping us and leaving us prostrate on the floor, looking for an emergency button to grab.

One of my go-to scriptures addresses our falling down incidents. "Rejoice not against me, O mine enemy: when I fall, I shall arise; when I sit in darkness, the LORD *shall be* a light unto me." (Micah 7:8, KJV; emphasis mine) There are two weights that pile on us when we have fallen and are sitting amid our tears in the dark. First our enemies, be they physical or spiritual, are rejoicing.

There was a news video that was broadcast after the mass murders of 9/11 that illustrate the rejoicing of our enemies. America, and most of the world, were in shock and disarray. The Twin Towers had fallen, the

Pentagon was aflame and a cornfield in Pennsylvania had become an unwilling grave for those heroes aboard an ill-fated jet liner. The video showed Osama Bin Laden and his evil murderers laughing and rejoicing over what they had done. That is a perfect picture of what happens when a Believer in Christ Jesus falls.

It is in times like that we need a knight in shinning armor to rescue us. President George W. Bush was our fearless leader who helped us get back to our feet when he perched himself on the pile of twisted steel and debris in New York, and declared for all the world to hear, that the people who took down our buildings, would soon hear from us. And they did!

The second weight is the darkness that drives the light out of our eyes and hearts. We feel alone and can't get our bearings. We reach out, as if blind, trying to touch something that will give us enough stability to regain our footing. The Apostle John understood our need for light in our darkness. He was the first leader to stand on the rubble of our lives and proclaim: "The Word (Jesus) gave life to everything that was created, and his life brought light to everyone. The light shines in the darkness, and the darkness can never extinguish it." (John 1:4–5, NLT)

When you fall, either through your own mistakes or through a hard push by life and/or evil forces, and you are driven to the ground in despair, look for the beacon of light that is Jesus. He will be searching for you as a shepherd scours the countryside searching for a lost and stranded lamb. Look toward the light and cry out to him. He will lift you up and place your feet on solid ground. Your enemies will stop laughing when the majestic King of Glory arrives.

Worry

I wish I did not worry so much about things that are out of my control. I know all the right answers about how to deal with worry. The bible is filled with admonitions not to worry and not to fear. My head knows but my heart often forgets. There was a song we use to sing back-in-the-day about worry. It said in part, "Why worry when you can pray? Trust Jesus, He'll be your stay. Don't be a doubting Thomas. Trust only in His promise. Why worry, worry, worry – when you can pray?" I've learned through the years there is a direct disconnection between worry and prayer. The more you pray, the less you worry.

Prayer tells your problems about your God. Worry tells you about your problems. Our prayers need to be filled with words of belief that God is able to deliver you from any and all circumstances. Praying releases a flood of faith that God will not desert you in your time of trouble. The Holy Spirit within you intercedes on your behalf according to St. Paul. "In the same way, the Spirit helps us in our weakness. We do not know what we ought to pray for, but the Spirit himself intercedes for us through wordless groans." (Romans 8:26, NIV)

Psalm 23 states that the shepherd's rod and staff will be comfort for us. The rod is an offensive weapon in the skilled hands of a shepherd. He can crush a scorpion with its tip or break the jaw of a lion with a well-placed power swing. The staff is a tool of safety for the sheep. Its crook can gently lift a wee ewe from the miry clay or quickly wrap around the neck of a unwary ram about to stumble over a dangerous precipice. "He lifted me out of the pit of despair, out of the mud and the mire. He set my feet on solid ground and steadied me as I walked along." (Psalms 40:2, NLT) The shepherd is always on guard watching over his flock.

The next time worry drives its spiny barbs into your mind, call out to the Great Shepherd to come to your rescue. He will rush to your side to save you and quiet your fears. He will tenderly apply a healing balm to your wounds and lead you to a quiet place of safety for your soul. "You have bedded me down in lush meadows, you find me quiet pools to drink from. True to your word, you let me catch my breath and send me in the right direction." (Psalms 23:2–3, MSG)

Worthy

"You paid how much to buy that?" Every person born on the earth since the invention of barter and dollars has heard that question asked. Things are worth what someone is willing to pay for them. Hence, the rise of internet sites like eBay, where you will find someone willing to pay just about anything to get something. Beauty, it turns out, is in the eye of the buyer.

What are you worth? Not how much money and stuff you own, but what value do you have to others? The answer to that question tells a lot about you and your true value. Most people place very little value on themselves, which helps explain, in part, the vast number of people addicted to drugs (legal and illegal), depression, and suicide. People don't feel loved or appreciated.

The good news of the scriptures is that God, in His love for you, has purchased you from the chains of sin and sorrow. The price He paid to have you as His prized possession gives you an idea of what God thinks you are worth. For example, what if your mother gave you her diamond ring right before she died. How much would you take for that cherished final gift of your mom?

God, in His love for you, had to decide how much you are worth to Him. He owns everything in the heavens and the earth so He's certainly rich enough to buy you. But what's the most valuable thing in heaven? Gold? Diamonds? Pearls? No, the most valuable thing in heaven is God's only begotten Son – Jesus. God believes you are so valuable that He gave the most precious thing He had in heaven to purchase you. He gave His Son to pay the price for you. "Do you not know that your bodies are temples of the Holy Spirit, who is in you, whom you have received from God? You are not your own; you were bought at a price. Therefore honor God with your bodies." (1 Corinthians 6:19-20, NIV)

So the next time you get down on yourself, try placing a value on Jesus, the Son of God, and understand that you are so valuable to God, that the price He paid to have you, was the life of His Son. Now, how much are you worth?

You Still Have Value

No doubt about it, we live in a disposable world. It costs more to fix most things that break then to replace them. Finding a technician that has the skills to repair an item is like finding the proverbial chicken's teeth.

But what about people? What happens when we break or get too old? Should we be cast into the rust bucket with all the other old and broken people? My dad had to spend the last two years of his life in a nursing home. I would visit him every morning to get his day going. I shaved him, shared breakfast with him, and tried to encourage him so he would know he still had great value to me. I remember sitting in my car every morning and crying before I went into "that" place to see him, and repeating the tears when I would leave. It was a difficult time.

There was a lady who was in the same nursing home as my dad. She would be wheeled into the breakfast area slumped in her wheel chair. She never lifted her head or spoke a word. But one day a most unusual thing happened. I was watching my dad slowly work his way through breakfast and started singing to him an old song of the faith: "When we all get to heaven." My singing is really bad but dad seemed to like it. As I was singing the little lady in the wheel chair was passing by. Her head rose from it's permanent sagging position on her chest, and she looked directly at me. She had the most beautiful crystal blue eyes I have ever seen. They flooded with tears of joy at the lyrics. Her wrinkled cheeks regained their youthful luster for a brief moment. She was alive again! When the song ended she asked if I would sing another one for her. From that day on, whenever she saw me, she would ask me to sing. I would kneel next to her chair and whisper a song just for her. Her ancient eyes would turn into glistening pools of joy for a brief moment. She once again had value.

There is a scripture that reveals our value to God. We may break down. Life may crush us. Friends and family may desert us. But God says: "A bruised reed he will not break, and a smoldering wick he will not snuff out."" (Matthew 12:20, NIV) You have value in the sight of God. You may be bruised or smoldering, but God bends down to sing over you. If you stop and listen you may hear the melody and lyrics: "What a day of rejoicing that will be. When we all see Jesus, we'll sing and shout the victory." Be encouraged, you still have great value!

Key Word Index

Key Word	Page
Abortion	7, 78, 292
Abundant	199, 203, 214
Abused	10
Accepted	10, 270
Alive	43, 185, 237
Alone	38, 92, 194, 201, 321
Amazing Grace	141
America	12, 27, 40, 101, 104, 180, 211, 278, 280, 296
Angels	38, 149
Anxiety	97, 242
Appreciation	97, 108
Authority	64, 135, 138, 284
Awe	17, 262, 300, 309
Azaleas	4, 115
Baptism	19
Beautiful	1, 4, 111, 116, 209
Beauty	100, 115
Bedrock	103, 205
Behavior	144, 206, 222, 275, 290
Believe	65, 74, 100, 135, 153, 236, 292
Believers	157, 239, 300
Bible	24, 261, 263, 300
Black Friday	38, 129, 280

Black Robe Regiment	27, 180
Blessings	30, 46, 231, 281
Blind	165
Boredom	57
Born Again	147, 178, 222, 257
Bucket List	94, 177
Calm	120
Card	216
Change	126, 213, 221, 228
Christianity	248
Christmas	37, 74
Church	17, 248
Commandments	275
Commitments	221
Compassion	3, 33, 146
Condemnation	90, 239, 244
Confusion	121
Constitution	7, 104
Control	162, 168, 305, 323
Creation	126
Cross	64, 144
Crucifixion	62
Dangerous	258
Darkness	320
Dark side	289
Daughter	32
Dead	43, 147

Death	12, 276, 283
Debate	236
Decision	54
Delight	111
Dependence	72
Depression	45, 140, 326
Deserted	24, 33, 48
Despair	48
Difficult	328
Direct	60
Directing	124
Direction	51, 60, 286
Discouragement	48
Doldrums	57
Doors	60
Doubt	194, 310
Easter	62, 64
Education	24
Elderly	328
Elections	27, 134
Enable	90
Encounter	234
Encouragement	2
End Times	69
Enemies	72, 80, 320
Eternal Life	65, 148, 153, 172, 178, 203
Eternity	264, 269

Evil	35, 228, 255, 269, 283
Excitement	17, 58, 249
Excluded	10
Fail	144
Failure	94, 256
Faith	72, 185, 256
Faithfulness	146
Fall	320
Fasting	80
Fear	224, 323
Fears	264
Feelings	85
Flying	314
Follow	91, 190
Forgiven	276
Forgiveness	94, 143, 256
Foundation	103
Fragrance	99
Free	239
Free Speech	29
Freedom	12, 42, 101, 104, 180, 195, 211
Friend	107, 268
Friendship	48
Fruitful	242
Fun	35, 243
Future	22, 314
Gentiles	272

Gift	131
Giving	113
Glory	115
God	10, 118, 120, 123, 188, 230, 296, 305
Good	129
Good News	189
Good Friday	129
Gospel	131
Government	105, 134, 137, 181, 278
Grace	110, 114, 140, 171, 239, 244
Graduation Day	25
Grave	64
Guarantee	145
Happiness	267
Healing	167
Heaven	152, 154, 178, 317
Hell	178
Help	107, 156, 224
Heroes	212
Holy Spirit	19, 86
Holy Week	62, 163
Honor	78
Hope	38, 48, 289
Hopeful	294
Hopeless	23, 224, 313
Hurricane Katrina	168
Hyper	171

Identity	303
Imagination	174
Increase	91
Independence Day	180
Integrity	183
Interest	54
Jesus	74, 185, 269
Jews	272
Joy	2, 213
Judgement	69
Kingdom	188, 261, 299
Law	89, 239
Leadership	190
Learning	193
Lent	15
Liberty	12, 40, 180, 195
Life	4, 25, 43, 198, 202, 287
Live	193
Living Water	304
Listen	92
Loneliness	200
Love	23, 204, 208, 294, 301
Loved	326
Mardi Gras	15, 35, 206
Marriage	204, 208
Meditating	175
Memorial Day	196, 211

Memories	37, 198
Military	196, 212, 284
Miracles	58
Money	113
Morning	1
Mothers	77
Mother's Day	79, 216
Movement	86
Murder	218, 284
Name	235
New Year	23, 221, 315
Non-resistance	139
Only child	200
Peace	38, 55, 247, 309
Perfect	207
Perfection	255
Plans	127, 174
Pleasure	108
Polls	236
Poor	10
Power	17, 227
Praise	163, 230, 232, 281, 303
Pray	41, 225
Prayer	40, 64, 96, 232
Preachers	263
Priceless	199
Primeval	35

Principles	41
Privilege	189
Promises	52, 300
Prosperity	96
Prosperous	31, 242
Protect	78, 205
Purpose	126, 128
Reality	165, 174
Redeemer	102
Refreshing	241
Rejoice	45, 243
Relationship	304
Remember	118, 158, 212
Repentance	20
Reputation	155
Rescue	156, 259, 321
Respond	92
Rest	92, 140, 241, 246, 273
Resurrection	43, 62, 64, 146, 185, 236
Revival	248
Righteousness	144, 259
Romance	301
Rules	275
Sacrifice	197, 251
Safe	60
Save	159
Saved	148

Saints	144, 253
Salvation	121, 255, 258, 269
Security	72, 124
Self-esteem	126
Self-reliance	193
Shelter	169
Sin	12, 15, 159, 206, 258, 265, 269, 300, 326
Sinners	144
Skeptic	147
Sorrow	267, 327
Soul	269
Spiritual Directions	52
Strong	310
Submission	139
Success	24
Suffering	157, 297
Surgery	149
Surprise	19
Taxes	113, 137
Teach	141
Tears	328
Temptations	265
Thankful	22
Thanks	119, 158, 217, 232, 246, 277
Thanksgiving	63, 158, 277, 280
The Word	184
Theology	172

Thoughts	213, 292
Tithe	113
Tongues	20
Tragedy	267
Transform	6, 132
Travelers	286
Treasure	32, 317
Trophy	154
Trouble	159, 230
True	262, 294
Trust	145, 162, 169, 225, 296, 316
Truth	27, 52, 184
Unbelief	224
Unborn	8
Unjust Laws	7
Unshakable	299, 309
Valentine's Day	253, 261, 294, 301
Validation	303
Value	326, 328
Volunteer	149
Wait	162
Waiting	305
Walk	286
Walls	272
War	269, 308
Warfare	312
Weak	310

Weapons	312
Weary	273
Wisdom	55
Women	78
Worry	175, 213, 323
Worthy	323

Scripture Index

Scripture	Page
Acts 1:4-5 NIV	21
Acts 3:6–8 NIV	59
Acts 4:33 NIV	17
Acts 13:38-39 NIV	256
Acts 13:52 NIV	17
Acts 16:25 KJV	243
Acts 16:30-31 NKJ	153
Acts 19:2 NIV	20
Acts 19:6 NIV	20
2 Chronicles 7:14 NIV	42
Colossians 1:22-23 NLT	254
Colossians 3:17 NIV	279
1 Corinthians 1:7 NLT	311
1 Corinthians 2:16 NLT	228
1 Corinthians 6:19-20 NIV	327
1 Corinthians 9:25 NAS	155
1 Corinthians 11:3 NIV	83
1 Corinthians 13:4-6 NLT	295
1 Corinthians 13:4-8 NIV	205
1 Corinthians 13:7 NLT	294
1 Corinthians 15:5–8 NIV	238
1 Corinthians 15:5-9 NIV	186
1 Corinthians 15:17–19 NLT	237

1 Corinthians 15:51-52 MSG	71
2 Corinthians 2:14-15 NIV	100
2 Corinthians 2:16 NIV	100
2 Corinthians 3:18 MSG	116
2 Corinthians 5:17 GWT	222
2 Corinthians 10:3-5 NIV	312
2 Corinthians10:4-5 KJV	175
2 Corinthians 10:4-5 NIV	228
2 Corinthians 10:5, NIV	293
Ecclesiastes 1:2 NIV	22
Ephesians 1:4 NIV	11
Ephesians 1:6 NKJ	11
Ephesians 2:3 NIV	287
Ephesians 2:4–5 NIV	148
Ephesians 2:4-6 NIV	44
Ephesians 2:8-9 NIV	207
Ephesians 2:14 NIV	272
Ephesians 3:20 NAS	214
Ephesians 4:18 NIV	148
Ephesians 5:25 NIV	82
Ephesians 5:31 NIV	209
Ephesians 6:4 NIV	83
Ephesians 6:12 NIV	313
Exodus 20:13 NIV	8
Galatians 1:4 NIV	260
Genesis 32:30 NIV	235
Hebrews 10:11 MSG	252

Hebrews 10:12b-13 MSG	252
Hebrews 11:40 NIV	256
Hebrews 12:27-28 NLT	309
Hebrews 12:28 NIV	262, 300
Hebrews 13:2 NIV	151
Hosea 11:2 NIV	31
Hosea 11:3 NLT	119
Hosea 11:4 NIV	31
Hosea 13:6 MSG	231
Isaiah 5:4 NLT	111
Isaiah 30:21 NIV	121
Isaiah 42:3 NLT	33
Isaiah 61:3 NIV	6
James 1:5 NLT	55
James 4:13-14 MSG	199
Jeremiah 29:11-12 NLT	225
Job 38:2 NLT	297
Job 42:3 NLT	297
John 1:4-5 NLT	321
John 1:14 NAS	115
John 4:13–14 NIV	304
John 6:68 NIV	191
John 8:36 NIV	14
John 9:25 NLT	166
John 9:39 NIV	166
John 10:10 KJV	178
John 10:10 NKJ	203

John 11:25 NIV	68
John 13:35 NIV	302
John 20:25 NIV	75
John 20:29 NIV	75
1 John 1:9 MSG	95
1 John 2:2 NIV	266
1 John 4:19 NIV	302
1 John 5:13 NIV	153
Lamentations 3:21-23 NIV	146
Lamentations 3:22–23 NIV	3
Luke 2:14 NIV	38
Luke 3:4-6 NIV	121
Luke 3:18-20	181
Luke 6:38 NIV	114
Luke 11:46 NIV	240
Luke 22:42 NIV	233
Matthew 5:6, NIV	81
Matthew 6:19–20 MSG	318
Matthew 6:25–27 NIV	315
Matthew 6:33 KJV	26
Matthew 6:33 NIV	316
Matthew 7:13-14 NAS	288
Matthew 9:36 NIV	157
Matthew 10:30 NLT	55
Matthew 11:7-8 KJV	182
Matthew 11:28 NIV	273
Matthew 11:28–30 MSG	93

Matthew 11:28-30 NIV	140
Matthew 11:29-30 MSG	194, 247
Matthew 12:20 NIV	329
Matthew 16:19 NIV	189
Matthew 16:26 NAS	155
Matthew 17:2 KJV	116
Matthew 24:21–22 NIV	169
Matthew 28:18-20 My Version	65
Matthew 28:18-20 NIV	65
Matthew 28:19 NIV	18
Matthew 28:19–20 KJV	220
Micah 7:8 KJV	320
2 Peter 3:10 NIV	67
Philippians 2:3–6 MSG	108
Philippians 4:4 NIV	46
Philippians 4:5 NIV	46
Philippians 4:6-7 NIV	46
Philippians 4:8 MSG	176
Philippians 4:8 NIV	48, 214
Philippians 4:8 NLT	39
Psalms 1:3 NLT	242
Psalms 20:7 NIV	73
Psalms 20:7-9 NIV	135
Psalms 23	241
Psalms 23	264
Psalms 23:2-3 MSG	325
Psalms 23:4 NIV	201

Psalms 23:5 MSG	61
Psalms 27:13 NKJ	145
Psalms 30:5 NLT	2
Psalms 30:11–12 NIV	2
Psalms 31:15–16 NLT	2
Psalms 33:12 NIV	98
Psalms 37:23–24 NIV	60
Psalms 40:2 NLT	324
Psalms 100:4 NIV	233
Psalms 118:24 NLT	231
Psalms 119:105 NIV	124
Psalms 139:5-7 NLT	52
Psalms 139:13-14 NLT	55
Psalms 139:13-16 MSG	126
Psalms 139:17-18 NIV	242
Revelation 3:8 NIV	60
Revelation 3:20 NIV	61
Revelation 22:17 NIV	141
Romans 1:11 NIV	131
Romans 1:15b NIV	132
Romans 1:21-22 NIV	132
Romans 5:20-21 NIV	172
Romans 7:7 NIV	276
Romans 7:18-20 MSG	290
Romans 7:24-25a MSG	291
Romans 7:25 NIV	244
Romans 8:1 NIV	244

Romans 8:1-2 NIV	90
Romans 8:25 NLT	307
Romans 8:26 NIV	324
Romans 8:28 NIV	128
Romans 8:28 NLT	230
Romans 10:9 NIV	144
Romans 10:9-10	270
Romans 12:17-18 NAS	184
Romans 13:1,3a NIV	285
Romans 13:4 NIV	139
Romans 13:13-14 NLT	16
1 Thessalonians 5:16–18 NIV	318

About The Author

Morris J. St. Angelo is the senior pastor of New Beginnings Church in Slidell, Louisiana. He is a graduate of the University of Houston and attended the New Orleans Baptist Theological Seminary. Most of his life was spent in the computer industry, from sending men to the moon during the Apollo missions, to CEO of his own nationally marketed computer software company. But his passion, that began when he discovered Christ in 1972, is living and sharing the story of Jesus and His unfathomable Grace with all who need God. Morris believes in the Finished Work of Jesus and salvation by faith in Him alone.

For more information about Morris St. Angelo and his ministry, please visit **www.GraceThoughts.net**.

If you have a testimony to share after reading this book or would like to contact the author please do so in email form at **info@GraceThoughts.net**.

www.ingramcontent.com/pod-product-compliance
Lightning Source LLC
Chambersburg PA
CBHW070526090426
42735CB00013B/2879